CREATIVITY RULES!

CREATIVITY RULES!

A Writer's Workbook

JOHN VORHAUS

SILMAN-JAMES PRESS   LOS ANGELES

First Edition

10 9 8 7 6 5 4 3 2 1

Library of Congress Cataloging-in-Publication Data
Vorhaus, John.
Creativity Rules! a writer's workbook / John Vorhaus.--1st ed.
p. cm.
1. Authorship.   2. Creative writing.   I. Title.
PN147.V67 2000   808.'02–dc21   99-057598

ISBN 1-879505-50-9

Cover design by Wade Lageose

Printed in the United States of America.

SILMAN-JAMES PRESS
1181 Angelo Drive
Beverly Hills, CA 90210

this one is for the writers

My goal in this book is to make you a more creative, productive, effective and satisfied writer. I'm confident that I can reach this goal— but not without your help.

CONTENTS

Acknowledgements

I've taught writing in 17 countries. In exchange for my service, I have received fees, thanks, free drinks, and life experience in measure beyond measure. I've also received a great deal of education; teaching the craft of writing in so many places has broadened and deepened my understanding of the common obstacles that writers face, and contributed directly to the strategies and tactics presented in this book. Writers everywhere have challenged me—through their struggles and their questions—to sharpen my focus and clarify my approach. The writers I've taught have made me a better teacher and writer, and I thank them deeply for that. If this book helps writers, then I will have done my job—with help from friends around the world.

So thanks to the writers, without whom this book would not have been possible.

Thanks also to

My wife, Maxx Duffy, for the title of this book, and also for the writer/editor road map; most of what I know about editing I learned from her.

Skye Dent, for the hopeful e-mail revealing the nickel in her hope machine.

Lost Lamb, for the scathing rebuke; how can I experience ego death if everyone keeps telling me how wonderful I am?

Katrina Wood, for sending me overseas.

Scott Guy, for the partnership notes.

Gail Morgan Hickman, for teaching me about premise pages and emotional core.

The Men About Town, for "Trivia for Idiots"; *nunc est verbendum,* my brothers.

Jim Fox, for his usual delicate touch.

My family, with whom I am blessed.

And Kate Moss, for her inspirational quote, and if she wants me to thank her personally, I do stand ready.

FOREWORD

by Jeff Arch

I thought I'd start out this Foreword to John Vorhaus' new book by telling you something that drives me a little bit nuts: You know how when a book comes out, and there's all this hype on the cover that promises to tell you the *SECRETS* to this or that? Whether it's success in the stock market or cooking a good brisket or the "secrets" to brilliant writing, somebody's out there trying to get your attention in a big way, and tell you just what those secrets are. Which sort of makes them . . . not secrets.

A great example of this is a greeting card that's always going around: On the front, it says, "The Secrets To Success." And then when you open it up, there are these gigantic letters, saying:

WORK!

Now, first of all—is that a secret? That you need to work to be successful? To me, the answer is pretty plain—because on one level, I truly think that anybody who works, with discipline and dedication, toward a goal they deem to be worthy, is already successful. But you and I know there are other levels than that. Look at writing, for instance, since that's what this book's about, and let's take it as a given that in order to succeed, you have to work at it. And then let's take a look at every writer who's really working at it, and ask them if they think they're successful—only let's define "success" this time in the crass commercial way that the *rest* of the world thinks of it. Especially your friends and the people in your family—and if you've been at this writing thing for a while, you know what I mean.

Then ask yourself—really ask yourself—if you think the difference between those two types of success is a *secret*. It might be something you don't currently *know*, and that's okay—because fortunately, this book you're thinking of buying (or borrowing) (or have just bought or borrowed) (but you'd better not steal it), can help you, in that there are a whole lot of things in here—suggestions, explanations, techniques and exercises, all delivered with patient and compassionate good humor, so that you can read them and try them and think about them as a means of getting better at what you do.

These things are called *strategies*. And guess what? Over the course of a career as a writer, you're going to need a ton of them. You need to know a hundred different ways to make something happen during those wonderful times when they don't happen by themselves. You need to know a hundred different ways to poke and prod and tickle your brain and your heart into working together to create something of value, so that it can get to an audience who will appreciate it enough to tell their friends. You need to know a hundred different ways to get started, a hundred different ways to keep going, and a hundred different ways to get to the end.

And that's what this book is about. More than anything, it's about strategies. Because where a lot of other tremendously worthy and worthwhile books deal with theory and explanation, the strength of this one is in John's ability to get you *doing* things, in addition to showing you how they're done.

Secrets? I don't think so. When I think of a secret, I think of something that people don't *want* you to know—and writing a book about it doesn't seem like a hell of a smart way to keep anything a secret. And that's not where John lives anyway—this is all stuff he's *determined* to pass on to you. Because if you know him at all then you know he's a born teacher—the kind whose enthusiasm for what he teaches is infectious and irresistible, in small doses or large. He's naturally playful, extremely willing to be silly, and urges us to do and be the same—or to try it, anyway, which anybody should do, if they're really serious about their work.

Ironic, isn't it—that the willingness to be silly can be an expression of how serious you are.

And that brings us back to *Creativity Rules.*

Now if you know John at all, or if you're already familiar with his work, then you're probably ready for a **Grand Sweeping Statement**, which I'll set off in bold italics, for the highly professional reason that I know how to do that on this software:

John Vorhaus is a lot like Costco.

"Whoa," you might say. And by golly, you'd have every right. But every once in a while, it's time to take a stand—and by the way, taking risks and taking a stand with your work is something John urges you to do, and shows you how, in this book. Still, I know what kind of water a person can get into by comparing another person—an *author*—to a chain of discount warehouse superstores which seem to be springing up like pod people in a B-movie. And Costco's one of the big ones, and since John's a lot like Costco, this all had better be good news.

But there's more—because not only will I stay on the limb I started out on, but I'll go even further and admit that I can compare John to a place like Costco, *without ever having been in one.* And no, it's not because I'm some yuppie-weenie-espresso-latte-capuccino-Nordstrom-Macy's-jerko snob. Mainly because I don't drink coffee and I don't understand Macy's and Nordstrom's either. What I *do* understand, clothing-wise, is catalogs. My wardrobe comes from the same catalog every time, and it consists of blue t-shirts, in the variety of short sleeve or long sleeve. They are the kind that look like you've already had them for ten years and have been sleeping in them for at least half that long, and I highly doubt they can be found in a department store—and even if they could, that means I'd have to go there, and department stores for me are like airless decompression chambers in that if I don't get in and out in less than ten minutes, things start happening to my central nervous system that can cause rattling in people's china cabinets up to three counties away.

I know what you're thinking here. You're thinking that the guy who's writing this Foreword is *really* stalling. Come on—writing about pod people, and blue t-shirts from catalogs, when neither one has any kind of connection to a book about becoming a better writer? Or does he have a point, and will he get to it someday? Well, if you read the book, you'll learn a simple way to measure that. So, if you really want to know, then go and read the book, and I'll wait here and you can come back.

Okay? Are you back? You got the answer? Good. Now we can move on. Because now you know that the way to test for stalling is to *ask if what you're writing moves the story forward or not.* Or, in this case, the FORE-WORD—and I use capital letters here, to compensate for not getting paid.

The point of *this* story is how John's book is a lot like those Costco places, and just to prove I *wasn't* stalling (and thanks to those of you who stuck with me and especially thanks to the ones who wrote or called in to come to my defense), I can and will give you the three main reasons right now:

Why John Vorhaus—his book, anyway—is a lot like Costco:

1. There are more things inside than you could possibly need.
2. The thing you need, they have.
3. It's a bargain.

There.

Now. Did I need to put you through all this other stuff, just to get to that? No! Resoundingly no, and I think you know that. On the other hand—and I say this using hyphens—did I enjoy going off on a tangent like that? Absolutely! You're *supposed* to enjoy your writing, and John even says so in his book. So, going off on subjects like catalogs and discount warehouse superstores and all that other stuff *wasn't* stalling. Instead, I was wasting your time *intentionally*.

Because John let me.

Look, you're probably a writer because you've been receiving subtle clues all your life that you're—well—different. And if you've been a writer for any longer than five minutes (and sometimes it doesn't even take *that* long), then I'm sure a lot of people have stepped up to remind you how hard it is, and what the odds are, and all the other stuff that comes with the totally whacked out and brainless decision that they're trying to talk you out of. So the *real* question should probably go a little more like this:

Will this book make me a better writer?

And of course, the answer is, No! How can it? It's a book! Go ahead, sit it down at your computer and see how many pages it comes up with. Or, try a better question—like this one, maybe: Would *reading* this book and doing all the exercises like there is absolutely no to-morrow if you don't, because you're a committed writer who is looking for more tools, more approaches, more ways of setting up and evaluating your work, get you closer to your goal of being published, produced, pack-aged and booked on *Letterman*?

All of the above. Except *Letterman*. The director gets the talk shows.

One more thing and then I'm out of here. Every sum-mer I get to speak at this conference in Glendale, Cali-fornia, which is extremely close to Hollywood and has clean hotel rooms under five hundred bucks a night. It's an annual event where writers from all over the U.S. and a few other countries come to spend three days in the heaven of Being Understood by other writers, teachers, and Real People in the Business, who make themselves accessible and try to help them crack the code that we're all so desperate to crack. On this particular year, I was the wrap-up guy—the last speaker they were going to hear before they all had to check out of the hotel and say goodbye to each other and go their individual ways—away from the rarefied atmosphere of a commu-nity of kindred spirits and back to the worlds they knew, and the worlds that knew them.

So they were a little nervous. And that's what I talked to them about. *How* to go home, *how* to carry on in the face of all the daily obstacles and resis-tances—real and manufactured—and still produce the kind of work that would lift them out of the anonymity that all writers, even the ones who aren't anonymous anymore, face every day.

But before I got into all that, I asked a general question of the group. I reminded them that I was the last presenter they were going to see, and that if any of them had come with a hope or an expectation of the conference that hadn't been met yet, they should speak up now, and I would do what I could to make up the difference.

One guy called out immediately. "You can buy my script," he said, and we all had a good laugh about it while I tried to have him thrown out. But the thing was, he meant it. The guy had come a long way, and had invested a decent amount of money and time and energy into this conference, and had admittedly set the bar pretty high by expecting to leave the place with a sold script.

So I walked off the stage and went over to where he was sitting, with his script right there in front of him, and I took out twenty dollars and gave it to him. "There," I said. "Now you can go home happy." And I took the script and went back up onto the stage and did the rest of my speech, while he sat there and must have wondered if what just happened was a good thing, or a joke at his expense.

But here is the moral of the story. For all writers certainly, but especially for screenwriters:

1. If all you're thinking of is selling your work, you're not thinking far enough.
2. The director will still get *Letterman.*

Enjoy this book. I know you will.

Jeff Arch
October 1999

INTRODUCTION

> *"To say this book is about me (which is the main reason I was uncomfortable—me, me, me, me, me . . . frightening!) is ridiculous. This book is not about me."*

supermodel Kate Moss,
talking about her book,
Kate: The Kate Moss Book

This book is about you. It's about the writer you are, and the writer you want to be. It's about your dreams, aspirations . . . your fears. It's about your war, and if you don't know what war I'm talking about then maybe this book isn't about you, and you can stop reading now.

Since this book is about you, I'd like to ask you a question, and since we're just getting started I'll make it multiple choice.

Why do you write?

A - *easy money*

B - *can't hold a real job*

C - *just want my voice to be heard*

D - *just sort of feel like I have to*

If you answered A—*easy money*—you're either deluded or perverse, both treatable conditions. If you answered B—*can't hold a real job*—at least you're being honest. If you answered C—*just want my voice to be heard*—you deserve honor and respect, and possibly prayers. If you answered D—*just sort of feel like I have to*—you're in the big fat majority here.

Many writers feel like they have no choice. They write because something named or nameless inside them *makes* them write. They often feel frustration because nothing they write seems to quell or quench the urge within. So they answer D—*just sort of feel like I have to*—but they're not necessarily thrilled with their selection.

And that's the war, the writer's war, the constant struggle between the urge to write and the dread that it won't go well.

And war, as we know, is hell.

But writing isn't hell, not always. Sometimes there are moments of pure glory, and without those moments we'd just walk away, no matter how much *have to* we had. Those moments are the addiction condition of writing; they make us act like rats in a subtle and devious laboratory experiment: *press bar, get treat.* We don't try to quit. We have no real desire to quit.

And *choice* is the reason why.

Even though we may feel we have no choice *but* to write, we always get to exercise the choice of *what* to write. That's the best part. That's where the glory lives, as well as the buzz—the buzz of having the pure power to choose. A power that no editor, publisher, producer, partner, loved one, critic, boss, client or buyer can ever take away, not truly. You might modify your choices to serve other people's needs, but ultimately it's your brain that drives your hands that bring your words to life.

Without you and your choices, it's just an empty page.

So recognize your power and own it from the start. Own the right to start stories you don't finish. Own the authority to create characters you later kill off. Own the initiative to try forms of writing you've never tried before.

Own your control over the most basic issue: *What do I write right now?* Above all, own your right to be wrong on the page. Be confident in knowing that choices improve as information improves—and that wrong choices lead to right choices in the end.

You get to choose. That's what makes you a writer, and makes some other poor jlub a muffler installer instead. You choose; you discover and judge; you select. In sum, you create. By making choices.

The writer's war is the struggle to make choices without going nuts. Without second guessing ourselves, annoying ourselves, stopping or subverting or diverting ourselves. If we succeed, then we communicate our thoughts in a meaningful way. If we fail . . . sigh . . . we try again, because we're writers and we can't stop writing. But even if we succeed, we . . . sigh . . . *still* try again, because we're writers and whatever writing worlds we conquered last week just won't seem to satisfy us next.

It could be a long war.

How long? That depends. What would you take as a win? What would represent total triumph over the forces of imperfect process and ongoing writer's angst for you? Writing a best-seller? Selling a screenplay? Having a steady writing gig with a weekly paycheck and health insurance? Publishing that collection of short stories? Releasing a CD of your songs? Posting a web page?

Please write down your response. I don't intend to do all the work around here.

Whatever writing goals we have, they all have this in common: If they're big goals, they're hard to swallow whole. We can't write a manuscript or a screenplay in a single sitting, and plainly it's unrealistic to try. While I'm no known fan of reality, I am a fan of practicality and, especially, efficiency. I can think of many strategies more efficient than trying to swallow a big goal whole. Strategies that I've thought of recently comprise the bulk of this book; ones I haven't thought of yet will not be presented at this time.

Meanwhile, back at the war, we find that we're assailed on all fronts. Procrastination creeps through the lines. Doubt occupies the low ground. Bills come flying in like bullets. Enemy personnel are constantly on patrol, trying to seize or kill our time. Metaphorical land mines (the worst kind!) block our path and also our Path. Inner terrorists lurk. Even the terrain seems to be against us:

> *Who put the delete key so far away? Why is it so hot in this room? When did my back start hurting?*

Then again, as wars go this is a fun one because you really can't get killed, and you *do* get to call the shots in a way that people who have only the desire and not the drive envy. Just ask the muffler installer. I'm sure that he (or she—this book provides equal opportunity for pronouns) would tell you that there are some terrific darn stories in muffler repair, if only one had the drive to write them all down. She envies you your war because war, albeit hell, is not dull.

So go out there and get bloody—okay, or anyway sweaty. Work up the kind of good creative lather that comes from putting hours into the task—waging the war—and finding that you're advancing on some fronts.

They may not be the fronts you expect.

But this battlefield is fluid; you never know where you're going to make your breakthroughs. In fact, given that creativity often involves taking yourself by surprise, you can expect to make breakthroughs in unexpected places. Especially if you're expecting them.

Expect the unexpected? Is that what this book's all about?

In a sense. There is a phenomenon that's common to writers, the *where did that come from?* feeling or sensation which washes over us when we see our writing take on a life of its own. You bury yourself in a writing project for an hour or a day or a week or a month or a year, and later you look back and wonder *where did all that come from?* That's the magic of writing: *I know that I wrote all the words, but they don't all seem to have been written by me.*

There's either a logical or a mystical explanation for this. Logic tells us that if we work on a project long enough with our conscious mind, eventually our subconscious mind starts to pitch in too. Mystics tell us that creativity is bestowed upon us by higher powers, and by writing we put ourselves into a place where higher powers can act. Which explanation is right? Whichever one you like.

They serve the same end.

If you take the logical approach, you'll spend more time writing in order to derive more benefit from your subconscious partner. If you take the mystical approach, you'll spend more time writing as a means of positioning yourself to receive the gifts that higher powers bestow.

Either way you win, because either way you're going to spend more time writing.

And *that's* what this book is all about.

To be a well-informed and confident writer, you have to write *a lot*. To write *a lot*, you have to be a well-informed and confident writer. How do we resolve this paradox? How can we work toward being the kind of writers we want to be in advance of having the necessary confidence and craftsmanship to move forward. How do we build strength?

Gradually. By degrees.

You start by pretending that you're not completely ignorant and ill-informed, and move your writing forward a tiny bit on that basis. Having moved your writing forward a tiny bit, you now have a little more writing experience to draw on. This experience gives you new information and new confidence, which you feed right back into your writing process, like a not-for-profit corporation feeds its income right back into research and development, or like a mama bird feeds half-digested worms down her babies' throats. Additional writing gives you more experience of yourself as someone who can do a writer's job, and also gives you more skills for doing that job. Each time you confront recurring writers' problems (motivation problems, story problems, logic problems, detail problems – oh, that list is long) you're incrementally better equipped to solve them than you were last time through. Eventually the war starts to go your way.

I've heard this said: If you want to improve your writing, write more; if you want to improve a lot, write a lot more. This is a useful suggestion, but it begs one key piece of strategy. Not only do you have to *write more*, you also have to *study* yourself and *experience* yourself as the writer you are, and the writer you're becoming. This wedding of *write more* and *study your process* moves you toward a well-informed and confident place. A place where a writer can get some real work done.

Take a long view of the war. You won't win it overnight. You may not win at all. You might never close the gap between the reality of your writer's life and the fantasies you create and sustain in its name. That's all right. You don't have to win the war; you just have to keep winning battles. To do that, merely keep writing and keep watching yourself write. You'll get better; it's a given.

Life is long. If you're still drawing breath, you still have time to be the kind of writer you want to be. Here's the kind of writer I want to be: *a better writer today than I was yesterday.* That's a reachable goal. That's something I can do. You can too. It happens automatically if we just keep writing. Well hell, that's all we really want to do anyway. All that could possibly stop us is lack of capability or lack of nerve. And *these* are two problems that the mere, sheer act of writing solves as well. Do anything long enough and you're not a rookie anymore. Skill builds confidence—confidence builds skill. Unless you feel you already have too much of both, strive to add to your store.

Words on the page.

Words on the page.

Words on the page.

I'm telling you, that's all it takes. I feel like I'm trying to sell you a diet supplement, *guaranteed to shed pounds!* It just *can't* be that simple. But it is. Really, it is.

Whether you're a rookie writer (or even a pre-writer) or a veteran, I hope and trust that this book will give you some new strategies and tactics that you can use in your war. But in the end my best advice boils down to this: Take small steps, and take as many as you can.

It doesn't take forever to get good, but it does take time, and it does take work. If you imagined that you didn't intend to harvest a single word you wrote for even five years, you'd be giving yourself a decent apprentice-ship to serve. You'd certainly keep your expectations in check.

But whose got that kind of patience? *I want the harvest right now. I want to be good from the start.* Okay, fine, but contemplate this: You don't have to *be* good to *get* good. Choose to learn. Choose to have patience. Choose to serve the writer you'll be in the long run. That's a place where a writer can stand, and that's a war that a writer can win.

November, 1999
Los Angeles, California

CHOICES

good writing

bad writing

recording reality

filters

she's deeply confused

good writing

What is good writing?

In grade school it was keeping the letters between the lines. In junior high, good writing equaled good spelling, plus the arcane skill of diagramming sentences. In high school I heard that the classics were good writing, but the classics put me to sleep. In college they said that good writing was all about conflict. I disagreed; they gave me an A.

So what's good writing? Right away we see that there are lots of right answers. *Hamlet* is good writing—but so, in the proper context, is "there once was a girl from Nantucket." What's good writing? Here's one answer:

Good writing equals honesty plus style.

It's a notion. Let's throw it out the window and see if it lands.

To start, write something honest about yourself or someone else. Just a sentence or two, or a paragraph or two; a simple human truth.

First, though, how do you plan to tackle the exercises in this book? If you have a word processor, you can open a file and label it "workbook." If you have a cocktail napkin you can label it "workbook" and use that instead. Results may vary. In all events remember that this is a workbook, and you'll really only get out of it what you put into it. At minimum, you may use the space provided. Any time it's time to write, you'll see one of these:

So here's me being honest.

I can't seem to get anything done today.

Now here's you being honest.

Now here's me being honest with style—a specific style we might label *fabulism* or *lies.*

> *First the pencil broke. Then, when I went to sharpen it, I stubbed my toe on the ottoman. "Damn ottoman," I muttered, which put me in mind of the Ottoman Empire and off I went to the library to find out more. When I got home, the phone was ringing, and since I realize that my opinion* does *matter, I spent the next half hour answering yes/no questions on subjects ranging from movies I have seen to my taste in maple syrup. Finally, just as I settled down to start writing, a clot of space aliens burst in and abducted me. That's the third time it's happened this week.*

Same information. Same truth. All I've done is lie it up. That's one way to apply style: simply lie it up.

Take a whack at it. Be honest with style through lies.

There are all kinds of ways to apply style. You can lie, as mentioned, or encode as poetry, inject humor, invent new words, exaggerate, allude, be bold, or use a dozen other strategies that I encourage you to think of now.

And notice that you attack the task in stages, first being honest and next applying your choice of exciting styles. This is beyond useful. It's fundamental.

Good writing breaks it down.

When you can link a simple human truth to a dynamic display of words, you may or may not be in the realm of good writing, but you've certainly acquired the knack for tearing things in two. Instead of needing to make some great problematic leap into "good writing," you have a simple system to follow: *First do A, then do B.* Try it a couple of times and get the hang of it. First do A, *be honest*, then do B, *apply style*. Notice which types of style you choose to apply. We tend to select the ones we like best or feel more comfortable with.

Now you have a simple, effective way to test your work. Why founder on the question of what is good writing when instead you can ask of the sentence you just wrote, *"Was it honest? Did it have style?"* In the light of this clear-eyed appraisal, you might want to go back and change what you wrote. That's fine. Good writing is subject to change. Because . . .

Good writing comes from rewriting.

You've heard it—read it in books like this—a million times before. But think of what this means. If good writing truly comes from rewriting, then *interim drafts don't matter.* This should set us free.

Let's see if it does.

Write a paragraph about anything at all. I'll tell you now that in about 30 seconds you're going to rewrite it, so don't sweat what you write. For ease of use, select and apply this style: *vernacular.*

> *Jeffy looking for trouble? Not even. Me and Jeffy, we're sack guys, not stick guys. But MacWorter, he can't let Jeffy skate, not after what happened at the bank. Man, don't even ask me about that.*

Now rewrite it. First clarify what you want out of the rewrite.

I want fewer words and more direct threat to the storyteller. Notice that I'll get a much different result with this clarification than if I decided to want, say, verbosity and literary pretension instead.

> *Jeffy? No shot. No way MacWorter lets him live, not after the bank. I saw it slide sideways. They'll smudge me when I tell. And I know I have to tell.*

Was your second paragraph better? If yes, here's why: Once again, you tore the task in two. First you wrote something, then you rewrote it. I don't have the specific math on this, but two small problems are usually easier to solve than one large one. Any time you get stuck, remember that you always have the option to break things down. It's the prime strategy for getting unstuck.

Plus there's this: When you wrote the first paragraph, you were flying kind of blind, but when you rewrote it, you had the *specific and direct experience of the first draft* to draw on. With every draft, you learn, and each draft informs and enlightens subsequent drafts. This is true for all forms of writing, from greeting cards to novels, from song lyrics to screenplays. It's no wonder the work improves; there's always a more experienced and better informed writer doing the rewrite.

So disconnect from interim drafts. Stop asking if they're any good. Questions of quality are *utterly irrelevant* to interim drafts. Now write—and then rewrite—another paragraph. Tell yourself exactly what you want out of your rewrite. The more precisely you can articulate the problem, the more quickly and efficiently you'll arrive at a solution.

It's easy to feel lost when you have instruction without information. *"Write another paragraph?"* *What does that mean?* You'd likely feel less lost if I said instead,

"Describe the contents of your medicine chest" (okay, do that) or "Write about your hobby" (do that too.) Without specific direction, you have too many options. We must make choices to narrow our options down.

I'd love to make your choices for you—writing is easier when it's just fill-in-the-blanks. But you need to make the choices, because that's what writing is all about: generating, sorting and controlling *choices.*

Your ally in all of this is the *arbitrary choice.* Writing tasks, especially in early stages of development, are dynamically driven by the arbitrary choice.

> *Should I write an 800-page philosophical*
> *magnum opus or an advice column or a*
> *comic strip or a fortune cookie or an*
> *obituary or a short story? Do I want*
> *choppy sentences? Sentence fragments?*
> *What about rhetorical questions? Should I*
> *write in the third person? Bare my soul?*
> *Hide behind wit? What?*

The choice—forever and for always—is yours. And here's a secret: *The choice doesn't really matter at all.* Any writing is good writing if it adds to the store of things you know how to do with words. Learn to make arbitrary choices quickly and confidently, and you'll come away with the ability to make things up on the fly. Does this contribute to good writing? You betcha, because . . .

Good writing is *imaginative.*

Imagine something. Write it down.

I'm sitting in a fountain. People are throw-ing coins at me. They think I can grant wishes. I wish they'd go away. Eventually they do. Son of a gun, it turns out I can grant wishes after all.

Writing on this level is pure discovery. You grab the first image that pops into your head—*pow! fountain!*—and hurl yourself into that image. Next thing you know . . .

Making arbitrary choices also mitigates the fear of making *wrong* choices. On the level of pure discovery, nothing is at stake. When you work in this no-risk envi-ronment, you build a habit of fearlessness that you can then export back to your "big" writing. So crank up your inventiveness—here in this very safe work-womb—and let your arbitrary imagination run wild.

Also let it run long, because good writing is *volume*. This is not an invitation to bury your subject in sen-tences, but rather a reminder that all writing improves the writer. Generate a tremendous volume of material and, if nothing else, you demonstrate to yourself the ca-pacity for generating a tremendous volume of material. So try it again. Open the spigot of your raw imagination and let it flow for as long as you can stand, and for ten minutes more after that.

Okay, so good writing is imaginative. What else is good writing? Conflict. Conflict is good writing, or so the experts claim. I always had trouble finding conflict until I realized that it lived in this three-letter word: *but.*

> *I want to work*
> > *but*
> > > *my dog wants to play.*

"But" is a beautiful word. It opens the door to conflict. Someone wants something, *but* someone else wants something else. When a boy scout tries to escort an old lady across the street, *but* she doesn't want to go, that's conflict. When evil madmen threaten our way of life, *but* we stop 'em, that's conflict. What's the largest conflict you can think of?

> *Denizens of a universe want to annex the universe next door, but the residents of that universe aren't ready to move.*

What's the smallest?

> *Gil wanted coffee, but there was none.*

If you care whether Gil gets coffee, then that's good writing too because . . .

Good writing makes them care about the characters.

So they say. Then again, they also say . . .

> *Good writing is the simple expression of complex concepts. Good writing is entertainment. Good writing is instruction. Good writing moves the reader. Good writing challenges the reader. Good writing makes the reader want to keep reading. Good writing is easily understood. Good writing is a call to action. Good writing is fresh and original. Good writing is cause and effect. Good writing is art.*

So they say. So what do you say? What is good writing to you?

Good writing is any of these things and all of these things. Good writing is *what you say,* because everything you designate as *good writing* becomes a *target* for your abilities and skills. If you say that good writing is a delicate melange of poetic images, sly references to biblical text, and linguistic borrowings from Raymond Chandler, then that's what good writing is. You now know the target you're trying to hit, and you can set about hitting it efficiently, logically, and (dare we hope?) easily.

Finally, how about this shocker: *All writing is good writing,* because all writing scratches the itch. *All writing* scratches the itch. Everything else—quality, elegance, coherence, meaning, money, praise, fame—all that stuff is secondary, after the fact. After the specific fact of scratching that itch.

So what's good writing? Don't ask me; I still can't diagram sentences. But I can believe that all writing is good writing because all writing contributes to our experience, builds fodder for subsequent drafts, and, most of all, lets us keep scratching the itch. Sometimes it seems like scratching the itch is the only good thing *about* writing.

But at least we get to do that.

bad writing

Show of hands, who wants to write badly? We want to write well, but when we set that as our goal we're burdened by expectations and the fear that we might fail. On the other hand, if you set out to write badly, you detach from the need to write well and that, at least, should ease the burden of expectation. Let's find out. For ease of use, start with this strategy: *Alliterate the crap out of something.*

*Burt barely burned Bob's big butt behind
Barb's black-beamed barn before Ben bent
Burt's back backward.*

Is this bad writing? Well if all writing is good writing then it's not, but I vote it is. If I treat it that way—*bad writing, as such*—then I get to leave behind all the baggage I normally lug toward good writing. Which leaves me free to concentrate on this given challenge to my problem-solving ability: *Can I write like crud?*

Here's a good trick for bad writing: *Set a task; execute a plan.* (If you see that, once again, we're breaking things down, award yourself a gold star. If you recognize this also as a trick for *good* writing, you get two gold stars, extra credit and a study hall pass.) In the exercise above, the task was *over-alliterate,* and the plan was *throw a bunch of b-words on the page.* In the exercise below, the task is *write a run-on sentence,* and the plan is simply to *put off the period as long as possible.*

> *Trying to avoid the inevitable confrontation between his will and his desire, Ngokl climbed to the top of the castle wall and looked out over the green heather and he noticed that the setting sun was setting in the west, as usual, and Ngokl thought about how strange it would be if the sun set toward some other point of the compass instead, but he had to admit to himself that now was neither the time nor the place to contemplate shifts in the celestial norm, not when the king was approaching, which, from the look of the train of wagons and horses now nearing the castle walls, certainly seemed to be the case, so Ngokl set aside the conflict between his will and his desire, and went to meet his lord.*

Now you go. Use the same strategies or try ones of your own. Play twice, just because it's free. And freeing. The task of writing becomes pretty easy when you set the bar so low.

That's the beauty of bad writing: there are no wrong answers. And there are so *many* ways to write badly.

You can write nonsense . . .

> *"Cymophobia," nattered Leandra, her horsemint kugel clinging in an almost*

scorpioid loculus. Later, in the sea dahlia threnody, her eleemosynary cribwork yielded to Snell's law, and she divulsed.

➔

. . . or be derivative . . .

"I have a gun," said Joe.
"But you don't have the guts to use it," said Ed.
"Bang," said Joe's gun.
"Ooh," said Ed's gut.

➔

. . . wallow in lame analogies . . .

The cowboy jumped on his horse like a pogo stick with boots.
The writer sat at his desk like Truman authorizing the Bomb.
The pitcher threw his changeup like a pitch slower than his fastball.

➔

. . . or be repetitious . . .

Start to turn the handle by turning the handle. Turn the handle until the handle stops turning. Once the handle has stopped turning, stop turning.

→

. . . or . . .

→

. . . or . . .

→

. . . or . . .

→

Here's a letter I received in 1983 and saved since then, which shows you what kind of compulsive packrat I am. And by the way—sad to say—it was written by a college-educated American, and not intended as a joke. Honest.

> *Dear Applicant:*
>
> *I am sorrie that this letter is not Addressed to you personaly, but time does not afford us that luxery. We have not received an answer back from our first letter to you. It just might be that you did not receive it? In summary, what I ask was that you be very spacific, about the position you are applying*

*for weather it is full time or part time. The
letter also explained the difficulties that
arose in putting our publication together,
hopfully they are in the past. We have
scheduled an interveiw period, the week of
Aug 22, 1983. Please write and let us know
if this is a good good time for you, also
include the position you are seeling. Our
New Production Address is above.*

Sincerely Yours

*Osmalt Sumwalt
(name changed)*

That's some stinky bad writing—but I'm confident we
can do worse. The challenge here is to reproduce the
style, grammar and garbled syntax of this artifact. The
other challenge is to commit the creative energy it takes
to compose something so (minimally) large as a business
letter. (This might be a good time to jump from the
SPACE PROVIDED to a notebook or document file of
your own.) The other *other* challenge is to leave your
baggage behind. Remember, it's only bad writing, and
the worse it is, the better you've done.

Dear Tehcnical Support,

*I have been playing your comptuer game
PIPES for sometime now and I have
aproblem I'm hopping you can help me*

*with. When I reach the level of 23
(password=fooz_ I finding that it sticks.
rlet me say that I get a msg of "systme not
reponding' so that I have to over again
from the outside in, what gives? Maybe
please send me one new copy, thats not
not good such as thik one is. Or less tell
me what I am dowing wrong; Plus also
plese tell me what is the last level of the
game, is 23 near the end or is there meny
more to come, I would like to knw so I
don't spent all time playing game of not
every winning.*

*PIPS is good game, but working would be
better.*

Sinclery,

*Bangee Brumludgett
(name retained)*

Look, look, look, I know that language is code. I appreciate that we all have to encrypt our thoughts with
common structure, or communication breaks down. It's
so crucial for a writer to be *effective*. But sometimes its
fun to just have fun. Also, by writing badly we become
more attentive to language, and that's never a bad thing.

What would a badly written page in a teenager's diary look like? You can approach this exercise any way
you want, but if you're strapped for strategy, try breaking it down into these simple questions: *What is this teenager honest about? How does this teenager talk? What
are this teenager's conflicts?*

➔

Write a paragraph summary of a very bad movie.

> *BOZO'S GOLD. Party clown wins the lottery, makes daft investments, loses everything, freaks out, robs a bank, takes hostages, dies savagely. Former title: BOZO'S LAST STAND.*

➔

With a clear enough sense of task, you should be able to write at least something about anything. Could you give me 500 words of an article for *Amateur Surgeon Magazine?* Could you conceive your own magazine and write its table of contents?

➔

These are *stretching exercises*. They should be easy, and if they're not now, they will be with practice.

You could write this: *The wedding vows for a hopelessly mismatched couple.* Or this: *The obituary of a man of miniscule fame.* Or this: *Technical writing from a clueless technical writer.*

(It's a challenge to my inventiveness to challenge your inventiveness.)

Write a Christmas letter. You know, one of those *Skippy broke his leg in August* deals. Make up the family, make up their history. For style, pursue a subtext. What grim secret is this family hiding?

> *Last summer we drove to Yellowstone*
> *Park, where everyone had a great time.*
> *Little Sally learned a valuable lesson about*
> *not teasing the bears. Now she's learning*
> *to write left-handed.*

Suppose I were in the market for travel trash, some pulpy paperback I could read on the plane. Can you give me a tawdry title and three cheesy paragraphs of a back-cover blurb?

The neighbors are complaining about your 4 a.m. bagpipe practice. They've written a threatening letter. It so happens that you are a sociopath. What letter do you write in response?

Now set your own task. Conceive and execute your own bad writing.

After practice, when your muscles are tired and sore, but in a good way, you look back and realize you really haven't suffered. Somewhere in the middle of the workout you even lost track of time. And if you feel stronger after your workout, it's not because the muscles are any darn bigger (they are, a tiny bit) but because you darn *used* them. You used them for a long darn time. So therefore, *bad* writing is *good* writing because it's a good workout.

And what could be bad about that?

recording reality

Great things happen when you start to record reality. You build creative skills, writing skills, and problem-solving skills. Plus it's fun.

Recording reality is a *text generator.* Use it to create new material for stories, plots, characters, scene descriptions, op-ed pieces, comic non-fiction, stand-up routines, magazine articles, jokes, cartoons, tiny books of big wisdom, sermons, web prose, whatever. Also use it to help make creative choices and solve problems in material with which you're already working. And don't worry too much about whether you draw upon outer reality—the world around you—or inner reality—the data stored inside your head. In the sense that it's all information, it's all equally real.

To start recording reality, simply list things you could list.

> *food products, addresses, friends, religions,*
> *attitudes, films you love, things people*
> *collect, people who owe you money,*
> *people you know named Frank, crimes,*
> *magazines, government agencies, cigarette*
> *brands, items in a lady's boudoir, phrases*
> *containing the word "art"*

Now select an item from your list, and list what you could list about that.

THINGS PEOPLE COLLECT: *toy trains, poker chips, beer mats, kaleidoscopes, merry-go-round ponies, antique stoves, lucky charms, miniature scotch bottles, baseball cards, paintings, porno, CDs, grandfather clocks, AOL discs, autographs, pins, pens, pennies*

Now pick one item from *that* list, and list aspects of that thing.

ANTIQUE STOVES: *chipped enamel, spindly legs, rusty griddle, gas burners, dents, burn scars, warming oven, built-in toaster, caked-on grime, squeaky door, storage drawer, defunct brand name, spring-operated timer, analog clock, broken thermostat*

→

Suddenly you're three levels deep into detail. You've created a picture of an arbitrary landscape without much effort at all. And you don't have to stop there. You can go four, five, six levels deep into detail—as far as you need to go to find what you seek.

You'd think it would help to have, say, a real antique stove to look at while you're generating this list. But you don't necessarily need it. Simply bringing your mind's eye to bear on a thing will spawn a wealth of detail. It's merely a function of focus. And by proceeding in this orderly fashion from level to level, you can bring any arbitrary landscape to life.

What if your landscape isn't arbitrary? What if you set a specific target? How would it be, for example, to go three levels deep into a particular character?

> SANDY SWEETWATER *is an unemployed actress. Here's what I know about her now: She's friendly, energetic, loud, disorganized, scrappy, fit, brave, outgoing, witty, willowy, broke*

> BROKE: *can't afford head shots, waits tables, hates her boss, mooches cigarettes, crashes acting classes, grazes supermarkets for free food samples*

> GRAZES SUPERMARKETS: *favors Bristol Farms, avoids high-fat samples, hates flavored coffee samples, flirts with the meat guys, hangs with the stock boys, dives the occasional dumpster*

Try that with a character of your own.

And from here you can jump right into story. Just list some stories that items on your list could trigger.

> *Sandy finds a spy briefcase in a dumpster.*

*Sandy gets food poisoning from a bad
sample and sues a store. Sandy becomes a
sample girl. Sandy falls for a fellow grazer,
but they break up when they discover that
they turn each other "normal."*

Now you've got some choices, but the question re-
mains, which choice is the right choice? Easy. The one
you like best. Thanks to *Sandy falls for a fellow grazer*,
I now know that she doesn't want to be normal, and I
discover that I'm interested in that. That's the gold of
recording reality: Sooner or later you find stuff you're
interested in.

**If you're going to make arbitrary choices, please
make choices that please you.**

We call this "recording reality," but aren't we just
making it up? Hey, it was *real* thought, and now it's *real*
words. What could be realer than that?

Lists can address problems of plot—the vexing question of what happens next. Say I have Sandy Sweetwater
trapped in an alley with bad guys closing in, and I don't
know how to get her out.

First I generate ways she *could* get out . . .

*over a fence, up a fire escape, down a
manhole*

. . . and then ways she *couldn't* get out . . .

become invisible, snatched by aliens, fly

. . . ways that are clever . . .

> *bluff, confuse, distract*

. . . strange ways . . .

> *fake a seizure, speak in tongues*

. . . or strong ways . . .

> *beat the snot out of everyone, climb the*
> *side of a building*

The root of most plot problems is a simple *lack of information.* We don't know our story or our characters or our world well enough to solve the problem at hand. By recording reality, you have a way out of this box, because you can always generate more data. If you're stuck in a blind alley, *study the alley more closely.* Something's bound to turn up. Something always does.

These are some common nouns of the common blind alley:

> *loose chunks of asphalt, a gutter running*
> *down to a drain, cracks in the red brick*
> *walls, graffiti, old posters, potholes filled*
> *with water and scum, a dim lamp over a*
> *steel door with the word "laundry" written*
> *in English and Cantonese*

> *And the door opens.*

The door opens? Boom! She's outta there! In the end, all I needed was a door. But . . . a door . . . it was so obvious . . . Why didn't I think of that in the first place? Why did I have to spend all this time recording reality? Because the door was not apparent to me. Without actively focusing our attention on the scene we're trying to capture, we often can't see what's there.

Lists are slow. They're sloppy and wasteful. You generate a lot of data that you never, ever use. But lists are steady and reliable and they're always there. Obviously if you already have the answer you seek then you don't have a problem. But when you get stuck, isn't it nice to know that there's an orderly (though somewhat inefficient) way to get moving again? And really, can you ever have too much data? Just curb the urge to apply style. Recording reality is about information, not style. Keep your reality lean to keep the act of recording it brisk.

Generate a setting and record some reality there. Then take it three or four levels deep into detail and see what you discover.

When you can travel in a handful of instants from this . . .

> *tropical island*

. . . to this . . .

> *paper umbrella in a rum float on a dented
> metal table outside a Quonset-hut bar
> overlooking sailboats, squalls and some
> surfers who don't seem to notice the
> sharks*

or from this . . .

. . . to this . . .

. . . you've started to develop a skill: the skill of moving from the *general* to the *specific*. This skill will inject a certain energy into everything you write, because *specific detail* has power that *general detail* generally lacks.

If you're having trouble understanding a character, generate new detail about that character. If you can't get to the bottom of a thought, record the top and sides of the thought. If you're looking for an action to close a scene, just compile possible actions and select from what you find. It's easy and it's not magic. It's just recording reality. Try it with an element from one of your current writing projects.

Now think about a place you know very well, but not one you can see from here. Maybe it's a place you pass every day on your way to work or school, or maybe a different room from the one you're in now. Think about that spot, but really *think* about it, and visualize it as completely as possible. Now record what you see. Paint a full and detailed picture of the place you're trying to describe.

That's half-useful, but this is more useful: Think about an incident of human interaction you've been involved in. Think about that event and *really* think about it. Especially notice the underlying emotions, expectations, attitudes and strategies of the people involved in the incident. Now record as many of these as possible. Paint a full and detailed picture of the interaction you're trying to describe.

You can record emotion and intent and desire the same way you describe walls and windows and colors of paint. The difference is that emotion and desire drive stories, while walls and windows do not. You can get as good at describing emotions as you are at describing colors, and when you do you'll discover that what was once amorphous and vague is suddenly startlingly real.

We writers have all the information we need. Plenty enough to invent stories and characters and plots and situations and dialogue, plus opinion, instruction, humor, pathos, meaning, tragedy, truth, nuance and rhyme. All we need is better access. We improve access through practice. We improve writing by writing. Every minute you spend writing, you get better by the exact increment of time you spend writing.

Even if you're only recording reality.

filters

Even if you don't see yourself as a story writer or fiction writer, at some point you might like to explore characters. You can do this easily, just by creating and then examining the filters through which characters process information. These filters dictate how characters act, react, feel, think and choose. Here are some common character filters:

>*reckless, naive, restless, radical, loving, cynical, boastful, imperious, jaded, wounded, bored, fearful, bashful, efficient, distant, virile, relentless, cheery, cheeky, perky, dismal, forgetful, evil, fatalistic, optimistic, lustful and lost*

Here are some more:

If you have a character whose filter is *lost,* you understand intuitively how that character will behave. To deepen this understanding, just articulate (via recording reality) the things that a *lost* person might do.

>*Doug stepped off the bus and looked around. He shook his head, read destination signs, looked back at the bus, shook his head again, asked a stranger what city he was in, walked a few steps in one*

*direction, turned and walked the other
way, then stopped. "I don't," thought
Doug, "have a clue where I am."*

It's alchemy, transmuting perspective into event, simply by listing actions driven by a filter. Do this a couple
of times until you feel comfortable with it. Again let the
arbitrary choice be your friend. Start, for example, with
the filter *angry,* and see what you can find.

You can also easily invent characters as the sum of
several filters. Give me *boastful, forgetful and bored* and
I give you a senile pirate on jury duty. I give you *perky,
quirky and dim,* and you give me . . .

➜

filter + filter + . . . (n)filter = character

What is the sum of *nasty, sexy* and *selfish?* How
would that character behave?

➜

You can always find new characters where filters intersect. As you explore these intersections, do yourself a

favor and give yourself lots of raw data. And keep it nice and raw. Yes, you can select, edit, expand and contract, but why bother polishing what no ever sees? Just generate material and concentrate on what you find. Stare hard at your characters' filters. Learn how they see their world.

Using random filters we can gain a general understanding of our characters' attitudes and attributes. Using certain specific filters, we can gain a deep understanding of our characters' core sensibilities and motivations. Here are three key filters you can assign to any character.

- *controlling idea*

- *primary orientation*

- *fundamental question*

CONTROLLING IDEA. Each character has a predominant viewpoint, the focus of that character's action and thought. This controlling idea may represent the thing the character wants most or needs most or fights hardest for or against. It could be a thing he or she would die for.

Controlling ideas are powerful and uncompromising filters that strongly drive characters' actions.

Here are some controlling ideas.

> *Learn to fly. Save the farm. Get love. Graduate. Destroy all monsters! Catch the bad guy. Solve the mystery. Explore the unknown. Ski till dark. Drink till dawn. Climb that mountain. Flee!*

Take a look at some characters you're working with now and identify their controlling ideas.

JIM RAFFERTY: Collect everything!

MEGAN MOORE: Win the World Series of Poker

VIC MIRPLO: Don't get caught

Or make a new character, simply by taking a controlling idea—*go veggie*—and building around it.

Carmine Pasquale's doctor just told him to alter his diet or die. Now Carmine— lifelong libertine—struggles to make some painful lifestyle changes.

As you can see, this generates story as well as character. You can reliably find story where controlling ideas collide and conflict.

It's party versus study and no holds barred when Cory and Melody move in together on the next episode of "She's Deeply Confused!"

Controlling ideas can also be less large, just the character's basic way of relating to the world. If a character's controlling idea is *take no shit,* you can expect her to throw a drink in some sexist rudehead's face. If a character's controlling idea is *seek thrills,* you can expect him to try bungee jumping.

As a point of interest, what is *your* controlling idea? Mine is *surf strange waves.*

PRIMARY ORIENTATION. Ask your characters, "What are you?" The answer they give is their primary orientation. Primary orientation is your character's strongest sense of self-identity, the thing she builds her hours, days or life around. Typical primary orientations include:

> *parent, commuter, artist, builder, politician,*
> *activist, ethicist, philatelist, journalist,*
> *retiree, pirate, biker, boy scout, soldier,*
> *daredevil, cripple, hero, freak*

Others include:

Primary orientation predicts behavior. If your character's primary orientation is *cop,* his life has a basis in "cop logic," and you can expect him to behave like cops behave. If your character is a star surgeon, she'll follow surgical procedure. What would an alcoholic do with a day?

> *His eyes opened on an empty bottle. When*
> *he moved the rest of his head, the bottle*

spun to the floor. As his head followed, he concluded that he had been drinking last night.

As with controlling ideas, you can also start with a primary orientation and build a new character around it.

I'm a man of God. I'm the maid of honor. I'm a hermit. I'm a widow. I'm a cheer-leader. I'm a lady. I'm in recovery. I'm a terrorist. I'm a con artist. I'm a magician. I'm a veteran. I'm an Olympic gymnast. I'm alone. I'm insane.

As a point of interest, what is your primary orientation?

Primary orientation provides a context for the controlling idea. Private detectives follow clues as a function of their primary orientation; each case they take becomes their controlling idea. Stories start to get juicy when there's conflict between the controlling idea and the primary orientation. *A con artist falls in love.* His primary orientation tells him to run more cons, but his controlling idea urges him to *get that girl.* The juicy story is his struggle to do both.

Investigate the link between primary orientation and controlling idea. Report on what you find.

FUNDAMENTAL QUESTION. Characters also derive actions and behaviors from fundamental questions, the basic human concerns that we all share.

> *Am I okay? Can I survive? Do I have what I want? Can I get what I need? Do I feel fulfilled? What if they don't like me? What happens next? What do I want to be when I grow up?*

Record some fundamental questions. Then record *yours*.

Characters can become enslaved by their fundamental questions, because these questions often cloak secret fears, and some characters will do anything to deny those fears. I'll show you what I mean.

First, attach a fundamental question to a character.

> *"Am I respected?" wonders Xavier.*

Then see how that character responds; that is, generate detail through the filter of Xavier's fundamental question.

*Xavier wears expensive clothes, fusses
with his hair, boasts, picks fights, talks
down to people, talks about people behind
their backs, becomes gregariously drunk,
picks up the tab, lies about his career,
drops names*

➜

Xavier fears that he's not respected, and that fear drives his actions. Seeking validation, Xavier orients all his behaviors around his fundamental question. Xavier may seem a little sick and twisted, but your character doesn't have to be sick or twisted to have actions driven by fundamental questions. Consider Marie.

Marie wonders if her tumor is benign.

She's not sick or twisted, just unfortunate, and her fundamental question now is *will I survive?* What can we predict about her?

*She'll have meaningful talks with family
and friends. She'll spend time in denial.
She'll reminisce. She'll act out. She'll feel
rage. She'll cover up her pain. She'll be
reckless.*

Some—or all—of these predictions will be wrong. That's okay. Wrong data is still data, and information you end up not using still goes a long way toward clueing you into your character's nature and intent.

In any event, you now have a choice of powerful filters, and dynamic predictors of behavior. Say you're trying to write about a drug addict. His controlling idea is *get high*. What would he do to get high?

His primary orientation is *junkie*. How does a junkie function?

His fundamental question is *will I score?* and his fundamental fear is that he won't. How does deal with this?

As we saw earlier, characters come to life where filters intersect. Using the three filters of *controlling idea, primary orientation* and *fundamental question,* you can discover in an instant what is essential about the characters you create.

- Controlling idea: *get everything.*
- Primary orientation: *rock guitarist.*
- Fundamental question: *am I loved?*

Based on this information, what sort of actions can you predict for this character?

Now make up one of your own, and predict that character's behavior.

Controlling idea:
Primary orientation:
Fundamental question:

Don't worry too much about the labels on things. *Is that an action or a behavior? Was that a question or a controlling idea?* The labels don't matter. Only the content matters. And the content only matters in terms of where it leads. In this case, content leads into character, and into character may be some place you'd like to go.

she's deeply confused

You can create characters out of *any*thing. You don't even need to start with a character at all, not even so much as a name. You can derive character through the filter of found language. Yes, it's true.

I have on my desk a theater playbill, and I extract verbatim from its *Who's Who*.

> " . . . *burst onto the scene* . . ." " . . . *for which she won* . . ." " . . . *most recognized for* . . ." " . . . *co-starred with* . . ." " . . . *other regional credits* . . ." " . . . *last seen in* . . ." " . . . *played on Broadway* . . ." " . . . *currently appearing in* . . ."

These phrases are artifacts of a particular language, the language of the theater playbill. Taken together, they create a *voice*, and you can use this voice to construct a character. Simply ask yourself who, in the world of your imagination, fits within the boundaries of the language artifacts you're examining. Then apply your (newfound?) inventiveness to the task of filling in the details of that person's background and state of being.

> ***SANDY SALTWATER*** *is perhaps best known as Sandy Seabed in television's* She's Deeply Confused. *After studying theater at Brown University, Sandy moved to New York, where she appeared in* Trevor, Trevor *(Pub Theater) and played the dual roles of Eve and Anna in*

Palindrome *at the Pepper Rep. Her film
credits include* The Legend of Sleepy
Hollow III *and* IV, *and* Gossamer Wings
for Showtime.

Try that.

Fabrication can be fun. With nothing at stake, we enjoy godlike serenity as we endow our characters with history and ambition, triumphs, vanities and hidden
agendas. This kind of fabrication is also useful, in that it
presents you with characters where before you had only
empty space—characters you'd be highly unlikely to derive by other means.

Now I'm skimming a copy of *Victoria Magazine* and
grabbing language from it:

> " *. . . a gift for her daughter . . .* "
> " *. . . you and Mother have long ex-
> changed beauty secrets . . .* " " *. . .* 'Dear
> Grandmother' *is a book you'll want to
> share . . .* " " *. . . Mama's kitchen was
> heavenly . . .* " " *. . . the mother-daughter
> team creates fresh-scented lavender
> lotions . . .* "

Can you guess who reads this magazine? Can you
create such a reader? Can you craft a letter to the editor
from this reader? Oh yes. Yes and yes. Simply attach the
voice of this magazine to the voice of an imagined
reader.

Dear Editor,

Ever since Mother passed, I've been trying to fill a great hole in my life. Today I saw your magazine for the first time, and from the cover story forward—"A Mother's Dying Wish"—it spoke to me. Believe me when I tell you that I stood in the bookstore weeping, just weeping . . .

Artifacts of language are everywhere: in sales catalogs, newspapers, web sites, handbills, junk mail.

When you're strapped for creativity, you can always borrow from what already exists.

Try it. Grab some text from a magazine, cookbook, or high school yearbook, and distill its language. Then cast a character from the voice you find.

There's a relationship between the reader and the printed word that amounts to a mutually reinforcing reality. *Guns and Ammo Magazine,* for example, sends the message that "guns and ammo are way cool" to people who already believe in the coolness of guns and ammo. This direct reflection of the reader's reality is directly how a magazine stays in print.

And that's useful to know if you write for magazines. You'll have much greater success *selling* to magazines if you pitch articles or story ideas that *directly reflect* the readership's preconceptions. Sorry if this sounds cynical, but which article is *Guns and Ammo* more likely to buy: pro gun or pro gun control? You can study artifacts of language to discover a magazine's or newspaper's point of view.

You can also learn more about yourself by examining the language choices you make. Here are some things I have said at one time or another.

> *A lie is not a lie if the truth is not expected. If I don't believe it, it isn't true. There's a fine line between insanity and minority opinion. What you see depends on where you stand. If you can't be right, be loud. I think we can all agree on the nature of consensus reality.*

Taken together, these artifacts of my language reveal me as someone who likes to question reality. Once you've made (or acknowledged) such discoveries about yourself, you can then export them into characters as a means of bringing those characters to life.

> *Harley Boone never signed on to the whole calendar thing in the first place. At the age of eight, he invented his own year, including holidays. When he tried to skip school to honor the Feast of St. Spreservus, counseling was recommended.*

And what might some other holidays in Harley Boone's year be?

Thus you can use your personal vocabulary to create character. If you imagine that you don't have a personal vocabulary, just explore your microculture—that set of experiences and memories that you share with a spouse or lover, friends, family or co-workers. These experiences and memories often come with language attached. For example, I have a friend whose father hands out hundred-dollar bills at Christmas. Because Ben Franklin's portrait graces this bill, it has come to be known that every year dad "Franklins" the kids. Any character who Franklins his kids is a character you can learn and know and use.

Record some of your personal vocabulary now, then create a character who fits that voice.

Characters you create from borrowed language have a borrowed feel. But characters who spring from your own language or history will be more authentic, because their voices come from within. They will also have the advantage of being uniquely your own, and thus much less likely to be cliched or derivative.

I seem frequently to invent characters with such personality traits as *obsessive collector; avid amateur poker player; shortcut taker; angle shooter; inventor of new words*. These traits mirror my own, and I find them easy to assign to characters. When we project our real selves onto our characters, those characters come more quickly and effectively to life.

Does this mean that all characters are or should be a direct reflection of the writer? No, of course not. Otherwise, I'd have to write middle-aged bald guys all the time, and never get to write spunky young women. But consider this: There is always an intersection between what's real about you and what's real about the characters you create. Find that intersection, explore it and write about it, and you can be confident that your characters will think, act and speak in authentic ways.

What characters do you write about most frequently and most effectively? If you can't answer that question, answer this one instead: What are your personality traits? What would happen if you pasted them directly onto the characters you're working with now?

Yes, this requires a certain minimum level of honesty on the part of the writer. You simply can't assign aspects of yourself to your characters unless you're willing to acknowledge and accept that those aspects live within you. This is a problem. I love, as I've mentioned, to write about obsessive collectors, but I can't do a good job of it unless I admit that *I'm one too.*

What would you rather not admit to yourself about yourself? Now go and build a character out of *that.*

Okay, by now we're pretty sure that we can create character out of anything that's left lying around. We can do the same thing with story.

As an obsessive collector, I happen to collect, among other things, Internet artifacts, those ephemeral renderings of reality that float around in the ether and occasionally tumble into my e-mail box. You've seen them: urban myths, jokes, scams, actual newspaper headlines, bad country-and-western song titles, and imponderable questions like, "How high is sea level?" I quote here from a collection of . . . well . . . mind-bogglingly stupid behaviors.

- *Trying to keep warm in freezing weather, a heavily clad 50-year-old man huddled over his paraffin heater. Accidentally overturning it, he set himself on fire. Screaming in pain as his clothes were engulfed in flame, he ran out of his hut and jumped into a nearby reservoir, where he sank like a stone and drowned.*

- *A psychology student rented out her spare room to a carpenter in order to nag him constantly and study his reactions. After weeks of needling, he snapped, and beat her repeatedly with an axe, leaving her mentally retarded.*

When I first read these, I thought, "Man, you can't make that stuff up." Then I thought, "Sure you can." *Then* I thought, "Let's give it a whack."

- *A man tried to kill himself by running his late-model sedan into a concrete wall. He forgot that his car had an airbag, which inflated, leaving him injured, but alive. En route to the*

> *hospital, the man seized control of the
> ambulance and attempted to crash it
> into a wall. He missed his target and
> flipped the vehicle, killing two para-
> medics. He walked away unscathed.
> And was hit and killed by a police
> cruiser speeding to the scene.*

That's a whole story—beginning, middle, and end—
all derived from an exercise in mimicry. Try it now. You
know how stupid people can be.

Just as you can create characters by poaching from
your own language, you can invent stories and situations
by aping *your own style*. Simply project your own voice
onto a character, and then devise a situation which natu
rally conflicts with that voice.

> *Jon had a wisecrack for everything. Birth,
> death, religion . . . Jon had something
> clever to say. And Jon was fine until the
> day he met a woman who wasn't dazzled
> by his quick wit. She wanted to know his
> well-defended heart, and Jon felt it wasn't
> wise to expose the cracks in that.*

What do friends say about you? What do you say
about yourself? Take one of those elements, project it
onto a character and propel that character into a story.
Don't worry whether the story "goes anywhere." In the
next section we'll explore the simple problem-solving
tools that can take a story from its beginning, over the

hurdle of middle, and on to a satisfying end. In the meantime, just notice again how easy writing becomes when you have a precise, well-defined task to attack.

Notice also how far outside the realm of "magic creativity" we now stand. Simply use what you have on hand, and your creative well can never run dry.

Story

sequence

What is story? Here's one answer I've heard, and maybe even it's true:

Story is a sequence of events.

Let's start with that, and see where it leads. First, write a sequence of events.

> *A woman walked into a library. She went to the stacks and found the book she was looking for. She took the book to the check-out counter and checked it out. Then she took it home and read it.*

Write another. Don't concern yourself with whether the sequence makes compelling reading, or even makes sense. Just speed from the *beginning* to the *end* of something as quickly and economically as possible.

> *A guy stopped to get gas. He gave the attendant ten dollars, pumped ten dollars' worth of gas, used the restroom, and bought a Pepsi and a package of pork rinds. Then he left. The end.*

Okay, that's a sequence of events, but not much of a story. So next let's throw another element into the mix: *surprise.* Now we have this:

Story = sequence of events + surprise.

Write a sequence of events in which something takes a character by surprise.

> *A woman stopped to get gas. She pumped ten dollars' worth. Just as she was replacing the nozzle, a car drove by and exploded.*

But random surprise isn't enough. We need the sort of surprise that actively defeats the character's expectations, which we can identify as a function of her point of view. Once we know her expectations, we can assault them with a string of related surprises.

Start by selecting any point of view. I select *innocence,* and invoke a character with an innocent point of view. Next I predict how an innocent person expects the world to behave: *kindly, gently, appropriately.* To build a story here, I just attack that expectation. I start by asking *what should logically happen next?* and then have something—*anything*—else happen instead.

> *An innocent man walked into a bank.*

What should logically happen next? He should make his deposit or withdrawal and leave. But instead . . .

> *An innocent man walked into a bank. He found a gun on the floor.*

What should logically happen next? He should turn the gun in, make his deposit or withdrawal and leave. But *instead* . . .

An innocent man walked into a bank. He found a gun on the floor. He picked it up to turn it in, but the security guard mistook him for a robber.

What should *logically* happen next? The innocent man should drop the gun, clear up the confusion, make his deposit or withdrawal and leave. *But* instead . . .

An innocent man walked into a bank. He found a gun on the floor. He picked it up to turn it in, but the security guard mistook him for a robber and shot him dead. The end.

Now our evolving definition of story looks something like this:

Story is a sequence of events that defeat a character's expectation.

Write a sequence of events that defeat a character's expectation.

And then write another. Just for yucks or just for practice. Note the distinction between gratuitous surprise—

Suddenly everyone was hit by an asteroid.

—and character-based surprise—

He had been watching the stars for months, confident that all was quiet in near space. But one night the stars started to move.

—and build yourself another string of surprises that aggressively attack a character's point of view.

Remind yourself that quality doesn't matter. Then notice how your second and third efforts are better—or at least better informed—as a result of what you learned from your first or second try.

> *A prostitute walked along a tawdry boule-vard. A car stopped. She expected the driver to be a john or a cop, but it was some college kids on a scavenger hunt, and "hooker" was an item on their list. They snapped a Polaroid, and gave her five bucks for her trouble. Although she imagined herself to be hardened beyond hurt, the memory of the moment haunted her all night.*

We can see a future for development of this thin yarn. We can imagine it spun out to a dozen doleful pages in a literary journal, thick with rain-slick streets and chill existential winds. Or we can imagine it as the starting point of a **MAJOR MOTION PICTURE!** starring **SANDY SALTWATER!** as a hooker on the road to redemption.

And that's all we need right now: to see the start of something. I know I'm asking you to do some real work here, so I'll ask politely. Please try sequencing a bunch of simple stories until you feel you have the hang of it.

→

A cynical gal went on a blind date.

What should logically happen next? We can deduce from her point of view—cynical—that she expects to get stood up. So we defeat that expectation.

> *A cynical gal went on a blind date. Her date showed up.*

A cynical gal would expect the date to be a loser, so we defeat that expectation too.

Her date showed up. It was basketball's Michael Jordan!

I know what you're thinking. The minute basketball's Michael Jordan shows up, the story loses all credibility. Maybe, but we're not paying off on credibility here. We're paying off on bold, imaginative choices. And which story is intrinsically more interesting? The one where she dates a loser, or the one where she dates basketball's Michael Jordan?

> *A cynical gal went on a blind date. Her date showed up. It was basketball's Michael Jordan! Against all foreseeable odds, they fell in love, got married and lived happily ever after.*

Is a story really that simple? In its barest bones, yes. Try it. Then try it again.

As you do this exercise, fight the urge to over-explain. We don't now need to know how the scavenger hunt is scored or why the gun is lying on the floor of the bank or what set of circumstances drove basketball's Michael Jordan to accept a blind date in the first place. For every writing task there is an *appropriate level of detail.* When the map of your story is first taking shape, the appropriate level of detail is *the least detail possible.* Why? Because at a time when you're still trying to figure out if you even *have* a story, too much detail bogs down your thinking, obscuring the story's essence and essential quality.

Too much detail is an easy and somewhat fun trap. To fall in, just over-write:

> *A hooker walked down a street. It was a long street, a lonely street, with stoplights at either end, which in Spanish are called* semáforos. *The hooker wore snug hotpants made of "nether leather," a shiny vinyl material which reflected the glow of the halogen—no, make that mercury vapor—street lights. For no apparent reason she found herself thinking about the irredentists, 19th century Italian politicians who advocated annexing certain neighboring regions. Then, by free association, she found herself thinking about her dentist, whom she hadn't visited in years. The dentist's name was Babydoll Sedoso or maybe Penny Featherweight or maybe Olive Branch or maybe . . .*

It's a party, a detail party, and it feels like a party because it's creativity without cost. But it does impede the task at hand, the task of moving the story forward. So throw the party once for fun . . .

Then note the trap (maybe mark it with a big red flag, or a yellow one, or green or blue or checkered, or, wait, does it have to be a flag?) and move along.

Only make choices you need to make. Don't bother making choices that don't matter now.

Since our ultimate goal is to turn small stories into big ones, let's see what we can learn by taking some big stories and shrinking them back down to small ones. Recognize these classics?

- *Young striver feels trapped at home until his aunt and uncle are killed. Later he believes he has mastered higher powers, but in the end discovers that he can only master higher powers by surrendering himself to them.*

- *Children experience stifling boredom until a mischief-maker arrives and intrudes on their tranquility. Despite their best efforts to control him, he creates increasing levels of havoc, leaving them convinced that doom is at hand, but manages to return everything to normal in the nick of time.*

- *Young girl with huge thumbs finds
  herself the receipient of two gifts:
  physical beauty and skill at hitchiking.
  She becomes a fashion model, falls in
  with challenging companions and
  emerges with a new, mature
  philosophy.*

Did you recognize *Star Wars, The Cat in the Hat,* and *Even Cowgirls Get the Blues*? This is not just a party game (though it makes a fair one). There's actually some utility in it. When you boil down strong stories you get strong models to follow. You get to see what the good ones look like.

- *Spoiled southern girl who defines
  herself through others finds herself
  thwarted in love, challenged by war
  and tempered by heartache. Eventually
  she stands on her own.*

So boil a few down—ones you've read, seen or heard, or even ones you've written.

By this method we can see the essence of successful stories: At heart they're all just events strung together with the rope of defeated expectation. *Inventively* strung together, sure, but who can't practice being inventive? Especially if you keep your stories spare, to minimize what your ego has to deal with.

We can create story by attacking expectations. But it may be that attacking expectations is not a sufficiently refined tool. After all, a character's expectations can be attacked in countless ways. And the better you know a character, the more avenues of attack you can find. Caught between choices, how does a writer decide?

Same way the characters decide. By sifting information through a filter. In this case, the powerful filter of *theme.*

theme

Since the dawn of time, humans have used story to convey information. First it was cave drawings and fireside tales. Later came sagas, scrolls and stone tablets, Vedas and Upanishads, passion plays and illuminated manuscripts, comic books and dime novels, radio, television, film, 'zines, and interactive DVDs, all to convey information more broadly, effectively and clearly.

Stories yields information: where to find food, how to hunt, history, civics, ethics, and, in the case of word problems, even mathematics. Stories inform, in sum, through instruction. In *The Little Engine that Could,* we learn not to give up. In *Groundhog Day,* we learn that it takes a man of quality to attract a woman of quality. In *Macbeth,* we learn that you shouldn't listen to your pride, or your wife, when they tell you to kill your king.

List the lessons in some stories you know. Try to convey this information as economically as possible.

- *Titanic*   fight for love
- *Winnie the Pooh*   cherish your friends
- *A Tale of Two Cities*   sacrifice for others
- *The Gulag Archipelago* endure

Powerful stories are *all about* instruction, and if you want to write powerful stories, start thinking in terms of instruction now.

An instruction, strongly expressed as an imperative, is the story's *theme*.

And theme drives story all the way.
Here are some sample themes:

> *Be yourself. Drive safely. Respect others. Stay cool. Attack expectations. Trust your gut.*

Here are some other sample themes:

Here are some things that are not themes:

> *competition; big money; greenhouse gas; romance; war is hell; people are strange*

These are observations or opinions or states of being, but they're not calls to action.

A theme is a call to action.

The theme of this book is *let creativity rule!* What is the theme of the thing you're writing now? Also record some other themes you're interested in, or ones you've explored in the past.

A theme is not a theme—not in a sufficiently powerful story sense—unless it *takes a stand*. Theme is command. Theme tells people how to act.

To test whether your theme is framed with the appropriate urgency, ask if it can stand the weight of an exclamation point.

Get naked! Get free! Get well!

I'm not a pedantic man. I'm not:

> *1. A person who overemphasizes rules or minor details*

or:

> *2. A person who makes an inappropriate or excessive show of learning*

I don't ask you to express theme as an imperative for some fetishistic reason or even in an effort to shape how you approach your work. I just know that weak themes kill stories, and if you start with strong themes you'll evade that trap. So *start with strong themes(!)*

Some writers fail to approach story with appropriate urgency because they fear that if they take a stand—declare a strong theme—someone somewhere will bust them for big ego: *"Where the hell do you get off telling me how to think, Mr. Bigshot Writerman?"* Certain cultures actually pound this notion into people's heads. In Australia, you might be instructed not to *skite,* or brag. In Norway, you might encounter the concept of *janteloven,* which warns you not to imagine for one minute that you're better than anyone else.

I'm telling you *do* imagine for one minute that you're better than anyone else—or you'll never find the wherewithal to sit down and write what you urgently want to write. And if you don't urgently want to write it, why should anyone urgently want to read it? For the sake of better writing, imagine that what you have to say is actually worth saying. Take responsibility for your vision.

Some people can't find their vision. They simply don't know where to look for good solid themes. But themes are never hard to find. Here's a trick you can use to identify themes that are important to you. Just ask this question: *If you could teach one person in the world one thing, what would that one thing be?*

If you could teach one other person in the world one other thing, what would that *thing be?*

If you could teach . . . are we having fun yet? The thing about theme is that every single story needs one, which means that busy story writers need lots of themes—and productive writers *have* lots of themes. Through practice, good ol' boring practice, you get good at thinking them up. So *don't be bored!* (That's a theme.) *Think of more themes!* (That's another.) Here are some more:

> *Challenge yourself. Embrace change. Take a stand. Push the envelope. Invest wisely. Be strong. Grow up.*

And here are some more:

Are you sick of lists? I'm sick of lists, but computer programmers get sick of source code, and lists are source code for what we're writing here. So *stick with it.*

And here's a shocking advantage: The minute you take a stand, your writing gets better, and easier, because you suddenly have a strong, clear, aggressive point of view. Theme answers that brutal writer's question, "What do I want to say?" If you *start out* with that answer, you're hugely ahead of the game.

Suppose your theme is (I choose arbitrarily) *enjoy Las Vegas!* What sequence of events could convey that instruction?

> *Ben and Ariel drove out for Las Vegas at dawn. Along the way their car broke down. Tempers grew short and they had a big fight. By the time they reached Vegas, they were both wrung dry. But dinner and a show and a small win at the craps table made them feel good again.*

Declare a theme and write events in its defense.

Theme isn't always the first thing you get, nor is the theme you start with necessarily the one you have at the end. Sometimes themes emerge from the material as it develops. Often, themes change as a function of new information about the characters and the story you're trying to tell. I like to declare an unequivocal theme at the outset of development, but then stand ready to change the theme as the work unfolds. So, no, it's not required that you start with theme, but it's always a reliable *point A* when no other *point A* presents itself.

There's gold all around you. Any time you want a new story you can pick up one and examine it, just by thinking of a theme and some events surrounding it. Next we'll examine a technique to make that process quick and easy.

snapshot

To develop a story we need development tools. Development tools remind me of developer. Developer reminds me of darkrooms. Darkrooms remind me of snapshots, and a story, it turns out, is something you can convey in snapshot form.

A story snapshot is a small lump of text (a paragraph or less) that reverses a character's point of view.

Here's how it's done. First, invent a character and a theme, and assign your character a point of view opposite to the theme.

Character: *Nosmo King*
Theme: *joyfully break free!*
Opposite POV: *irritably repressed*

Next, collect data. Invent some behaviors for your character that reflect his or her point of view. This is the character's *pre-existing condition,* the state in which we find him before the story starts.

> *Irritably repressed Nosmo King drinks stiff martinis, which he doesn't even enjoy. He wears polyester pants and old gray boxer shorts. He lives alone in a windowless room and wishes he had the nerve to grow a beard.*

Now take what you have so far *(character, theme, point of view, pre-existing condition)* and use it to create a story. Tell your story in the simplest possible terms. Use minimal detail as you try simply to reverse the character's point of view.

> *Nosmo King met a girl. She challenged him to open his heart, and he did. In the end, he even grew a beard.*

Beginning and middle and end. No nonsense, no filler, not a speck, as they say, of cereal.

Now do it with a little more detail. This is still a snapshot, still just a paragraph or less that maneuvers a character to a place where he changes his mind.

> *Nosmo King lived in a windowless room. He shaved meticulously every day. One day a Girl Scout tried to sell him some cookies. He reacted rudely and she busted him for his bad attitude. Eventually they became friends. She became interested in* [something near to his heart]. *He gave her lessons in that thing. Soon she was good enough to compete. At a key moment, she suffered a crisis of confidence. But his faith restored hers. Of course she*

won. He was so proud, but remembered
that he'd lost the bet [go back and add
bet] *and would now have to grow a*
beard.

At the snapshot stage of development, it's okay not to
have answers. In fact, it's more than okay, it's essential if
you hope to avoid the detail trap. I don't, for example,
yet know what Nosmo holds dear. But I know it'll be
something eventually, so I earmark the area and move
quickly on.

When doing development work at this level, fight the
urge to pretty up your prose. Fight the urge to rectify. If
you see an element at the end of the paragraph which
needs support from an earlier event, you don't have to
go back and add that element now. Just leave yourself
a note. It's okay to leave notes. It's okay to have inconsistencies. Or sentence fragments. Snapshots aren't meant
to be pretty. They're meant to be useful. Their utility lies
in giving you a firm little glimpse of a story you might
or might not later like to tell in a more detailed form.

Keep your eye on your process. Notice where your
writing is fluid and efficient, and also where you get
stalled. Too much detail is a big bog, but other pitfalls
abound. You can get married to a pretty image and
fumble around endlessly trying to make it fit in. Or you
can get stuck writing toward a favorite joke or image
long after the joke or image ceases to make sense in the
context of the story. My biggest distraction is *frustration*.
No sooner have I taken a snapshot of a story than I

become frantic to know everything there is to know about the story *right now,* and way too frantic over what I don't yet know.

But what I'm looking for in this snapshot is a complex and subtle thing: *Authentic transformation in a character's heart.* I can't realistically expect to have information so key, so central, at this early stage. I barely know my character. Literally, we've just met. I can guess at a transformation, and I can sketch one out in the simplest terms, but that's all I can hope for here. I have to remind myself to be patient.

Take a moment to think about the ways you get stalled in story. What things impede your swift movement from beginning through middle to end?

When you're writing story snapshots like this, push through to the end, any end. Remember that it's only a paragraph. Don't care what it looks like. Don't care if it's vague. Don't care if it's lame. It's a snapshot. It gives you something to look at.

And it gives you a way out of a particular bind—the inspiration bind. Now instead of waiting for the story fairy to kick you in the head, you can kick-start your own stories anywhere, anytime, out of anything at all. Just follow these six simple steps to snapshot.

1. Invent a character.
2. Select a theme.
3. Assign the opposite point of view.
4. Identify a pre-existing condition.
5. Describe a transformation in three sentences.

6.   Expand it to a healthy paragraph.

That's a great deal of progress toward story in a very short time. We play again. I start, you finish.

> *Character:*   *Oona Poona*
> *Theme:*   *embrace change*
> *Opposite POV:* *traditionalist*

➔

I've worked this exercise in classes, and no two Oonas are ever quite alike. Usually she's a woman, because the name triggers hidden assumptions about words with feminine endings. Often she's a Neanderthal because her name sounds like grunts to some people. Who is your Oona? A farmer? A diva? A nun? Writing a snapshot is like doing preliminary detective work. You take minimal information *(she's a traditionalist)* and turn it into story *(she's a farmer struggling to save her farm.)* Remember that that is catch-and-release creativity; if you don't like what you catch, toss it back. *(No, she's not a farmer, she's a nun, and the convent just closed down.)*

It's also cut-and-paste creativity. Look what happens if you just change Oona's name. *Winston Cabot* would suggest a whole different set of story choices. **SLEDGE SLATER** points to other choices still. In all events, our freedom to create is enhanced when we treat story as a problem to be solved instead of some vague and awful voodoo.

Take another snapshot or a couple, until you feel completely comfortable spewing information onto the page in this way. You can't always work effectively with creative material while it's still inside your head. You have to put it out in front of you in physical form, where you can see it and study it and start to give it shape. A snapshot is a very small and preliminary iteration of that shape.

Some snapshots naturally develop more quickly than others. Don't waste time on the hard ones, and don't feel bad about moving along. By examining many snapshots quickly, you get a lot of information, a lot of "story stuff," for not much creative energy and no creative risk. For the sake of gathering that information, and for the rush that comes from this kind of work, it's worthwhile not to dawdle.

What you'll derive from a good, strong snapshot is a clear and powerful, simple and direct set of events driving your character from some frame of mind or state of being all the way to its opposite, and all in a paragraph or less. Remember to look for real transformation, because transformation is where it's at with snapshots.

Once you have a snapshot with real transformation, you're ready to move ahead. And in this instance we move ahead by moving back. To the pre-existing condition. Where a bomb's about to go off.

change bomb

What makes a traditionalist give up traditional ways? What makes a peaceful person fight for her life? Why would a hermit leave a perfectly happily hermitly life, move to Manhattan and take up residence in a department store window? There would have to be a damn good reason, and that's what we'll hunt for next: a damn good reason to change. We'll call this thing a *change bomb*.

A change bomb ignites a story by upsetting the pre-existing condition.

Start with a character and a theme, an opposite point of view and a pre-existing condition. Then hurl something big and unexpected (or small and unexpected) at the heart of your character's opposition to the theme. Your goal is to shatter or destabilize the pre-existing condition. When that happens, the story is underway. Here are the moments of explosive change near the start of some stories:

- *A sheltered country girl lived in fear of the world. One day soldiers came, mistook her for a boy, and drafted her into their army.*

- *A cranky spinster lived in splendid isolation until an injured stray dog demanded her attention.*

- *A boy never liked girls until a lively one moved next door.*

- *A muffler installer lost her job.*

Here are some more:

How many change bombs can you think of?

> *Fired from a job. Discovered a corpse. Husband/wife left/died. Avalanche! Love at first sight. New kid in school. Supernova! HIV test was positive. Treasure map! A rift in the fabric of space. Prison riot. Wish came true. Stock market crashed. Aliens attacked. New bride. Met a mobster. Committed a crime. War began. Moving day. Check bounced. Hostage situation. Religious revelation. Strange parcel. Wrong number. Traffic accident. Switched suitcases. New hairstyle. Baby on the doorstep. Crash landing! Evicted. Television broke. Water broke. Graduation day. Blow to the head. Shocking telegram. Nervous breakdown.*

How many?

Your choice of change bombs is informed by the genre within which you're working. If you're writing a country-and-western song, then "My wife done left me" works as a change bomb. If you're writing a soupy ode, the first leaves of spring might be more your speed. In a murder mystery, discovery of the corpse is often the change bomb. In a love story, it's love at first (or second or third) sight.

If you get lost in all this, let theme be your guide. You can always anchor the change bomb to the theme.

Character:	*Oliver Switt*
Theme:	*Get physical!*
Opposite POV:	*Couch potato*
Pre-existing	
condition:	*Overweight, out-of-shape college student Oliver Switt hates all sports. He's never broken a sweat in his life.*
Change bomb:	*An athletic new roommate moves in.*

Another way to plant the change bomb is just to ask *what does my character value most in the world and how can I take it away?*

> *A pro sprinter loses a leg.*
> *A top surgeon develops a palsy.*
> *A free spirit goes to jail.*
> *A pop idol loses his fame.*
> *A brilliant scientist loses her mind.*

You want your change bomb to be a vigorous event, and you can select such events through the filter of theme. If the theme is *cherish loved ones,* look for something that takes loved ones away. If the theme is *play to win,* start with a loss. Seek to turn heaven into hell. When heaven becomes hell, your story has a good strong start.

So then, if you want your story to be dynamic, let it *start* dynamic. Plant a change bomb.

After that, get ready to press the issue. With pressure and response.

pressure and response

Characters hate to change because it imperils their worldview. A hermit, presumably, thinks hermiting is pretty darn fine or he wouldn't have built his life around it. When you confront him with other people or with intimacy or responsibility, you threaten his core assumption that he's better off alone. He won't like that. No reason he should. He also won't change until you force him to.

The truth is revealed under pressure.

If you want your character to overcome a fear of flying, you have to confront her with her fear. She won't welcome the pressure. But you should. Because pressure is exactly and precisely what moves your story forward.

I'm a conflict avoider. Many writers are. We don't love confrontation in our lives, and we evade it in our stories. But if we make things easy for our characters, we give them no reason to change. Even if you don't like conflict, learn to confront your characters. Learn to put them through hell—the stubborn bastards—it's the only way to make them change.

Somewhere in your writing there's a character you love. Think about ten horrible things you could do to him or her. Be bold. Be cruel. Have fun.

I'm not saying be *evil* to your characters (unless that's your intention). It's just that, to take them interesting places, you have to make them pay, and you make them pay with pressure. Wherever you are in story, pressure should be present.

Look for types of pressure appropriate to the type of story you're telling. In a cop drama, you'd expect to see crime pressure and death pressure, political pressure or emotional pressure. In nervous-youth fiction you'd find peer pressure, sexual pressure, grade pressure, family pressure, doubt.

Name a genre and list types of pressure appropriate to that style.

Be broad in your definition of pressure. *Thrown from a train* is obviously pressure. *Nasty ingrown toenail* is not so obviously so. *Insecurity* is pressure; so is *drought*. What are the inherent or implied pressures in a story that interests you now?

Just by listing the types of pressures present in your story, you give yourself lots of new information about where your story might go. It helps when you get stuck. Instead of asking *what happens next?* ask *what new pressure can I introduce?* Here we go again, breaking a large, floaty, amorphous, useless question down into smaller, more precise, more practical ones. At the risk of stating the obvious, a question you can answer is more useful than one you cannot.

Now let's see how to move a story forward on the two simple strokes of *pressure* and *response*. Start by writing a new story as far as the change bomb.

> *Professional poker player Megan Moore was a steely shell, the textbook definition of cool. Nothing ever threw her off her game. Till the night she found a corpse in her car.*

Next, add pressure.

> *The dead man was a poker pro like Megan, as were two subsequent victims. Megan came to realize that someone was stalking top players.*

How does your character respond? What simple action does she take in hopes of solving the problem she faces?

> *Megan took her suspicion to the cops.*

What's the next pressure?

But the cops couldn't help her.

→

How does your character respond?

So Megan decided to solve the case on her own.

→

THE PRESSURE/RESPONSE PISTON! It's easy! Fun! You can play at home!

PRESSURE: Cory had a crush on the new girl, Rochelle.

RESPONSE: Cory asked Rochelle for a date.

PRESSURE: She laughed in his face.

RESPONSE: He ran away.

PRESSURE: She told all his friends.

Try it.

→

Now try it without the handles.

→

> *I was napping in a hotel room.*
>   *The maid knocked.*
> *I told her to go away.*
>   *She knocked again.*
> *I opened the door to tell her more force-*
> *fully, "Go away."*
>   *She came in and started vacuuming.*
> *I told her to stop.*
>   *She ignored me.*

Pressure should escalate. Each instance of pressure should be bigger than the last. By direct examination of what you write, you can easily test your material to see if pressure escalates.

> *I stood in front of the maid, indignant, and de-*
> *manded that she leave my room at once. She*
> *dropped the vacuum hose and kissed me.*

Do these actions represent escalating pressure? Are things worse for our guy than they were? If yes, move on; if no, fix.

I like creativity that reduces everything to simple yes/ no decisions. When I'm asking questions as basic as *does the pressure increase here?* I feel confidence in my creative process. I may not like the answer I'm getting *(No, you nimwit, the pressure does not increase)* but at least I can trust that the answer is valid. I don't have to get lost in choices.

And it's so easy to get lost in choices. There's no one right path through story. *A Tale of Two Cities* didn't have to be about London and Paris. It could have been about Moscow and St. Petersburg (or Tampa and St. Petersburg).

But if this is true—if there's always more than one right answer—how do you ever reach closure?

Simply return to your theme, and orient your escalating pressures around it. Theme is your train. Pressure is your engine. Use pressure to drive the theme forward.

Theme: *Get out of hell.*

> Pressure/response: *On the day of the big amusement park trip, the kids were cranky, mom was edgy and dad had a hangover headache. Traffic was murder. There was a long line to get in, and long lines on the rides. The kids got sick. The parents fought. Dad got drunk. Mom left the park early with the kids. Dad passed out in the bushes. Security guards found him. He started a fight and they had him arrested. She wouldn't bail him out. He spent the night in jail.*

Theme: *explore the unknown.*
Pressure/response:

Remember your reliable tests:
- Is this event bigger than the last?
- Is this event linked to the theme?

And just as you're broad in your definition of pressure, be broad in your definition of story. In the sense, for example, that a song is a story, you can build song lyrics on the platform of pressure and response. Consider "Waltzing Matilda." In the pre-existing condition, a jolly swagman is minding his own business by a billabong. The change bomb arrives in the form of a jumpbuck, which the swagman seizes. Now here comes pressure: the stockman and his rangers . . . and the swagman responds by jumping into the billabong and taking his own life.

In stories or songs (or scripts or comic books or anywhere else that authentic transformation takes place), you'll find that the cycle of pressure and response escalates to the point where events can no longer be contained. In fact, it's something you can write toward. Try it. Write a hunk—I mean a *hunk*—of pressure/response and see if you can make things spin out of control. Again, don't worry about the logistics or the mechanics of the thing. Just point your events toward a place of large culmination.

> *Dad got out of jail the next morning. He came home to find that his wife had put his things out on the lawn. He talked her into letting him stay. He promised he would change. But he was angry inside, and the anger did not go away . . .*

This place is an explosive place. A place where things go boom.

boom

How far should you take a story? Answer: all the way. Keep throwing pressure at your characters until your characters explode.

> *Dad was sullen. The kids were afraid. It rained all day. The house was hot and damp. Of course he drank. He fell asleep on the couch. He woke up to find Mom sneaking out with the kids. He locked the kids in a closet. Then he locked the front door.*

It doesn't take long for events to get out of hand. Not unless you stall. Not that I'm stalling, but let's stop here and talk about stalling.

> *He stared at her. She stared at him.*

There's passive stalling, where you let events move forward without pressure or conflict. Passive stalling happens when we don't recognize whether pressure is escalating or not.

> *He stared at her. She stared at him.*

There's also active stalling, which happens when we're actually afraid to commit to certain story choices. We stall in this way when we don't trust that the choice we're contemplating is sound, and we'd rather run in place than risk walking down the wrong road.

He stared at her. She stared at him.

But if you're operating at the appropriate level of detail, you don't have to fear the wrong road. You still haven't made any huge investment in words. Even if you make an unsatisfactory choice now, you can use the information gathered on the wrong road to deepen your understanding of the story. Yes, you'll have to backtrack later, but not that far.

He stared at her. She stared at him.

Stalling can be fun. If you're being paid by the word, stalling can be profitable. But stalling is a trap like detail is a trap. Fall into it once now, and get it out of your system.

To cure stalling, do these two things:
- Make each event bigger than the last.
- Don't fear the wrong choice.

> *She went for the phone. He went for his gun.*

I hate that story choice, plus it scares me. I find myself confronted with the challenge of writing a story I can't really imagine myself writing. *Who are these horrible people, and how did I get involved with them?*

You do this sometimes as a writer: scare yourself with your own words. Especially as pressure escalates beyond the point of your control. Don't be afraid. Not that you need the reminder, but nothing you write can hurt you, and everything you write adds to your skill, knowledge, and confidence. So accept the challenge you set for yourself, no matter what that challenge turns out to be. In other words, let your writing be exactly what it is.

And even if you hate your stories, *finish them!* Finish them all. Because beyond stalling there's stopping, where you just quit on a story because you hate all your choices too much. Look, everyone quits on stories. We all write many more beginnings and middles than ends. But we need practice with ends, all the practice we can get. So finish your stories if you can, at least to this level of detail. Even if you hate them. Even if they scare you.

If your story scares you, explore *why* it scares you. I'm afraid to write this story of horrible domestic violence because I worry that people will think I'm *dark*. To me, I'm just a writer exploring a dark story. I want the freedom to explore that story. I can have the freedom, but I have to *take* it, which means I have to not worry if people think I'm dark.

So what are you afraid of?

Okay so we have *theme, pre-existing condition, change bomb, pressure/response,* and now *boom*. What kind of moments go boom?

- *Quinn and Oscar kept digging until Quinn's shovel hit metal. They had found the treasure at last.*

- *The coach sent Graham into the game. And there was only time for one more play!*

- *Freyda flexed her mighty wrists and snapped the chains like toothpicks. Now there'd be some hell to pay.*

Boom happens naturally if you let it. When you feel you're coming to the end of the story, you probably are. Or try this: Just keep writing until you hit something that can stand the weight of the phrase *"at last."*

At last . . .

> *Randy confronted the killer.*
> *Dierdre surrendered to love.*
> *Lilian found her father.*
> *The election results came in.*
> *The jury returned with a verdict.*
> *The lovers said goodbye.*
> *The armistice held.*
> *The boy stood up to the bully.*
> *The rescue boat arrived.*

What other kinds of moments go boom?

I have been frivolous. I will continue to be frivolous. I will keep making loopy, arbitrary choices that I have no intention of exploring or exploiting. At this level of detail I can afford to. I can monkey around with characters, create them in instants, put them through hell, then throw them away. These stories don't have to work. These moments don't have to work. They only have to lead eventually to something that does work. But how can you walk down a path you don't walk down?

Be frivolous. Be arbitrary and contradictory. Change your mind. Start over. But above all, *keep writing.* Nothing else matters. Not quality, economy, efficiency, marketability, logic or sense. Only writing. Only that.

He pointed his gun at her.

I am extremely not happy with this choice. I can't foresee any outcome from here that I'll like. Will he kill her? Will she kill him? Will they somehow survive this moment and both live on in this sick hell unabated? No, that's not what I want. I want them to climb out of this sick hell and get well.

And, suddenly, I know what I want, which I hadn't known before. You often don't know what you want for your characters or your story until you confront yourself with choices you *know* you *don't* want. This is why you have to be loopy and arbitrary and unafraid. Because you get to the right answer by going through the wrong ones.

So make choices you don't believe in. Whip your characters into a frenzy. Any frenzy will do, even if it's not the frenzy you think you want. By this method you'll soon discover where you *really* want to take the story, because you'll realize exactly where you're at. And where we're at, exactly, is the brink.

the brink

Your character has come so far. She started out in opposition to the theme. You planted a change bomb which shattered her pre-existing condition. Then you drove her toward truth through a series of escalating pressures and responses. You made her life go boom. Now she stands at the brink.

What happens next?

> *She surrenders to the theme.*
> *She steps over the brink.*
> *She doesn't fall. She* flies.

Here's how it works.

Suppose your theme is *sacrifice for others*. Your character's pre-existing condition (in opposition to the theme) is *selfish old bastard*. You've planted a change bomb by saddling him with an abandoned AIDS baby. You've escalated pressure by driving a wedge between his responsibility and his peace. You've moved him by a series of pressures and responses toward greater loyalty to the kid. You've made him go boom by bringing him to a place where he has to choose between that child and his old selfish ways. When he chooses in favor of the baby, when he takes a selfless step at last, he has surrendered to the truth of the theme. He's stepped over the brink.

How does he feel at this moment?

Intensely, immensely relieved. The thing that he's been fighting against for the entire story—the source of all the pressure he's been feeling—is no longer his enemy, but suddenly now his ally. Instead of sapping his strength, the theme suddenly *gives* him strength, because he has moved—explosively, instantly—from discord to harmony, from opposition to acceptance.

At the story's peak, the character steps over the brink by moving from opposition to acceptance of the theme.

Opposition to acceptance. Think of your story—the whole entire thing—as a simple switch from opposition to acceptance of the theme. To make this change take place, merely heap pressure on your character until her opposition crumbles and there is no place left to go but into harmony with the theme. Under pressure, the truth is revealed. And that truth is this: *I was wrong.*

At the brink, there is a clear, definite moment where the character declares *I was wrong.*

What sort of *I was wrong* declarations might a character make?

- *"I was wrong not to trust you."*
- *"I was wrong not to love life."*
- *"I was wrong to accuse you of murder."*
- *"I was wrong to think I could beat this thing on my own."*

Remember that we started out, way back in snapshot, with the goal of seeing an authentic transformation in a character's heart. Here, at the brink, the transformation is complete.

Dad's rage boiled over. He started to squeeze the trigger. Mom looked at him in horror. Then . . . she sneezed. Has anyone sneezed in the middle of her murder? It broke the spell of his rage. He dropped his hand. He dropped the gun. It was over.

How do characters undergo explosive transformation in some of the stories you've written, or the one you're working on now?

- *A girl thinks she can do without her father's love. It takes his death and ghostly return, plus the threatened loss of their ancestral home, for her to see that she was wrong.*

- *A guy wants fame so badly that he masquerades as a reclusive famous artist to get his share. In his moment of explosive change he realizes that it's the art, not the fame, that matters most.*

- *A struggling fat boy feels like a loser until he scores the winning run in a big baseball game. Performing beyond his own expectations, he realizes that he's a winner after all.*

"I was wrong . . ." is such a fundamental template. In the *selfish old bastard* example above, we could

substitute Tom Cruise for *selfish old bastard* and Dustin Hoffman for *AIDS baby,* and get *Rain Man.* Or insert a grandfather and granddaughter, and get *Heidi.* In either case—in so many cases—the same insight switch is thrown: *I was wrong; I'm not wrong anymore.* Underneath so many of the stories you know and love, you'll see that the map is the same: a pressure-driven run from opposition to acceptance of the theme.

Think about that. Think about stories you know, or stories you've written, and try reducing them to a simple line of change from opposition to acceptance of the theme.

Recall that *theme* equals *instruction:* a call to action strongly expressed as an imperative, for the sake of teaching the reader or the viewer or the audience a lesson. When the character accepts the theme, it is presented to the reader as a lesson learned.

Build a brief story that leads to transformation.

> *A timid man led a cowardly life. One day he was mistaken for a world-class criminal and became the target of a massive police manhunt. To make matters worse, real criminals were after him too, trying to rub him out. Although every move he made scared him, the thought of dying scared him more, and he found himself growing stronger and more capable by degrees. At last he stood on a bridge. The only way to*

*save himself was to jump. He'd always
been too scared to jump. Now, suddenly,
he found that he was no longer afraid.*

We haven't talked about it for a while, but do you feel more comfortable putting words on the page now? I hope you do. We're up to big paragraphs, and we're making creative choices with a suddenness that might have surprised you a while ago. Really all we're doing is just making our thoughts stand in line. They're more productive when they're orderly.

Not all stories, of course, are transformational. But it happens that transformational stories have great intrinsic strength, and have demonstrated this strength over and over again since storytelling first began. If you want a powerful story, driven by a meaningful theme meaningfully explored, then think in terms of transformation. You won't go too far wrong.

In any event, now you know where you're headed: toward a knowable, definable brink. Driving your character toward a brink gives you a clear, firm sense of control over your own material. Once you see the brink, you can move toward it with confident steps. Yet again you free yourself from the burden of the problematic question *what happens next?* Just declare at the outset that the character's final act will be one of transformation. Then just explore the terrain until you find a path that gets there.

If you know all along that you're heading toward a brink—*even if you don't know what brink*—you'll have a reliable way to test your material en route. *Does this moment move my character toward a point of ultimate peril and transformation?* If yes, continue; if no, fix.

Peril. Are we talking about physical risk here? Not just. In the example above, our cowardly character faced a mortal brink. He literally had to jump off a bridge to save his life. But he also faced a psychological brink. To survive, he had to let go of fear, a long-cherished and well-invested worldview which had previously instructed him that "fearful is the way to be." That act represents acceptance of the theme *Let go of fear.*

Transformation covers a broad spectrum of human events. A person can surrender to love or kill a foe or own up to a mistake or leave a toxic relationship or close a toxic waste site or conquer addiction or find God or gain self-respect or a thousand other defining events, all in the view from the brink.

Write some brink moments. Don't worry about the stories that might precede such moments. Just get a feel for what it's like to see characters suddenly surrender everything they formerly held dear.

If you've ever tried to solve the puzzle of a maze, you may have discovered that it's possible to cheat by working backward from the end of the maze instead of forward from the start. This is due to the design of the maze: There are many dead ends and false starts, and only one right path. If you start at the end and work backward, you know without a doubt that you're on the right path. You can work the same trick with story. Start with your brink moment and work backward from there. If you postulate—arbitrarily—that your story ends with your character standing in the church saying *I do,* you can reliably predict that all the preceding pressures and responses *must* aim toward this church wedding.

Can't figure out where your story's going? Try asking where it's been. As an exercise, first write the end of a story, and then write a paragraph of events leading up to it.

Okay, we've taken a character to the brink. We've forced the character to face transformation. Now that that's happened, what happens next? Is he done? Not quite. There's one more move left to make. The move into the blessed beyond.

the blessed beyond

I'm teasing you. I'm teasing myself. Our story geography doesn't really require such grand overblown labels as *the blessed beyond*. All we're really talking about is *crisis, climax, resolution,* where crisis is *boom*, climax is *brink*, and resolution is . . . resolution is . . .

Well, maybe it is the blessed beyond. After all, it's the place where your characters get fixed or rewarded, or they find peace or love or rest—the journey's end, whatever the journey happens to be. It's the place where characters, having connected at last to the theme, reap the rewards of order restored.

> *Dad was arrested. This time he'd serve time. He didn't even mind. He saw it—if he dared to hope and dared to work—as the first step on the long road back to earning his family's love.*

Often in this type of story, the character's blessed beyond is simply *back home,* to the place (or relationship or state of mind) that he would have valued if he'd seen its value in the first place. What other kinds of destinations do we find in the blessed beyond?

- *The killers, at last, were dead.*
- *He put down his boxing gloves and walked away; his fighting days were done.*
- *Free from fear, she went on to exciting new adventures.*
- *Now he understood that no two people were alike.*

- *The sun came out; they had survived the flood.*

Write some moments of blessed beyond.

Then write a quick story leading up to one of these moments, and see how the blessed beyond fits in. In particular, look for the connection between transformation and theme.

Transformation takes place when the character learns the lesson of the theme.

The transformational story requires reward. If we expect readers to buy the theme we're selling, we must demonstrate a positive outcome for the character who allies herself with the theme in the end. This cements in the reader's or viewer's mind the utility of the theme: *Do this and you will get that.* Remember that story is instruction. The reward for transformation underscores the value of the instruction presented by the theme.

This doesn't mean that all our stories have to have happy endings; a character can be transformed and still have a melancholy conclusion to her tale.

> *The rebels put Sheila to death. Though she thought it was tragic to die young, she knew it would have been more tragic still to have lived a long life and never taken a stand.*

So then, to draw a fairly fine distinction, a story can have a positive outcome and yet not a happy ending. Please write a moment of blessed beyond that demonstrates this.

You can easily predict or discover the blessed beyond in any story, just by looking at the sort of rewards that acceptance of a given theme is likely to bring. Suppose your theme is *leave the past behind,* and your story involves a character who goes back to high school to face old foes. What sort of rewards can we expect him to get if he wins? Self-respect. The death of his demons. A new beginning. Now we know *where* the story ends; the rest is just *how.*

Or, again, turn it around. Thinking in terms of rewards first, you can build the whole thing backward. Postulate that a character's blessed beyond is *playing major league baseball.* Knowing where she's headed— knowing that her story isn't over until she enters her blessed beyond—you will naturally search for and select events of pressure and response that move her toward big-league ball. You can also backpredict her pre-existing condition. Just answer the question *how far from major-league ball can you get?* Then start her story there.

Try that. Build one backward.

I confess a deep prejudice in favor of transformational tales. I believe in them. I enjoy writing them, I enjoy teaching them, and I note these benefits:

- They're rewarding to the reader.
- You get to speak your mind in words.
- The act of writing a transformational story can be transformational for the writer as well.
- Transformational stories have a clear, simple structure.
- Transformational stories operate on an emotional level, which is where powerful writing takes place.
- On the other hand, there's nothing wrong with non-transformational stories. One of those might look like this:

> *The king of a small medieval land op-
> pressed his people to the point where they
> could not work. Crops went unharvested
> and the population, weakened by hunger,
> soon fell victim to plague. Although the
> king survived, his circumstances were
> diminished, and he never did know why.*

Another one of those might look like this:

In either case, recognize that you're writing a *certain* kind of story. It's always easier to write a certain kind of story than just *any* kind of story. A target that's easier to see is easier to hit, and a well-defined target is simply easier to see.

summary

My map is my map. It works for me because it reminds me to write from theme, and to write from a strong theme that seeks to inform and instruct. Your best map is the one that invigorates your writing and helps you build your stories most effectively. Take mine for a start, if you like, but don't forget to scrawl all over it. And remember that this is a map for a *transformational story*, a particular type of story that leads to a positive outcome, if not always a happy ending.

To review:

- *Story* is a sequence of events designed to convey information.

- The specific information conveyed is the story's *theme*, an instruction or call to action, expressed as an imperative.

- A character, plus his resistance to the theme, can be discovered and displayed in a *snapshot.*

- Story starts when a *change bomb* goes off in the character's life.

- The character enters a cycle of *pressure and response*, oriented around the theme.

- Pressure continues till the story goes *boom*—

- at the *brink*, where a character surrenders his resistance—

- and enters the *blessed beyond*, where he experiences the rewards of being in harmony with the theme.

It's not the only way to build a story, but it's one way, and it prepares us for the real work of story development yet to come.

DEVELOPMENT

bridge writing

premise pages

outline

'script

summary

bridge writing

Write a new one-paragraph story.

Now ask these questions:
- Does it have a beginning, middle and end?
- Can I state the theme?
- Am I still interested?

If all the answers are yes, you're ready to move up from paragraph to the next level of development. *Devhellopment,* some say, and it can be a brutal slog, but it's a trip we have to take.

It's a trip some writers skip. They muddle a story around in their beans for an unfixed length of time, and then blurp it onto the page in some would-be finished form of script or prose. They think they're saving time with this shortcut, but it's a false economy because the first look at a story always reveals problems, and if the first look is also the last look, the problems never get solved.

If you're going to develop a story, *develop* it. Explore the whole terrain of it. Experiment with outcomes. Take the time—make the effort—to get to the bottom of your characters, your theme, your world. Recalling that there's more than one path through story, are you sure you want to trust your first idea to be your best? A rigorous development process lets you test alternatives.

Rigorous development forces ideas to compete.

In the universe of ideas, only the strong should survive. Do you have a problem with that? Don't you want strong stories?

> *Yes, but how long is this going to take? I told my agent that I'd have something new by the end of the* [year, month, week, day.] *I'm falling behind in my existence as it is. And now you want me to step into strenuous development? I strenuously don't think so.*

How long will it take? Too long. Longer than you'd like, I bet. Certainly longer than I ever like. Sad fact. But the alternative is no better. Lacking real, orderly development, stories fall apart or hit dead ends and end up half-finished and set aside.

Writers often hear this advice: "Finish the outline first. Don't go to script or manuscript until the story *really* works." Probably every writer has ignored this advice at least once (including yours, alas, truly). Some never stop ignoring it because the plunge into script or manuscript seems less problematic than the trek through proper development. So maybe I'm just wasting words here, preaching the gospel of proper development. I should delete this paragraph.

And would, too, except to demonstrate a point. There's such a thing as *bridge writing*, the writing we do to help connect our thoughts. Once you've made your connections, you can go back and delete the bridge. But you often *can't make the connection without building the bridge first.*

Bridge writing is rough writing. Bridge writing is overwriting. With bridge writing it's okay to waste words. Bridge writing believes that words like to get wasted. Bridge writing feels no strong compulsion to be *right*. Bridge writing only wants to explore, and will penetrate any depth to discover the truth of a moment. Bridge writing doesn't care how long it takes, or how ugly it gets.

So this is me demonstrating bridge writing and feeling *damned uncomfortable* about leaving this rough writing unedited for your inspection. But, boy, you've got to be willing to write unedited words or you never get anywhere with development.

Wrong story leads to *right* story.

How're you ever gonna get to right story if you don't go through wrong story first? And how will you get through wrong story if you're afraid or unwilling to hurl words at the page?

Try overwriting something without a care in the world.

When you rewrite the mess, it becomes less messy. But *less messy* isn't the goal of development.

The goal of development is to reveal the story to the writer. Pretty doesn't enter into it.

Use bridge writing throughout story development. Treat all the words between here and the final draft as mere keystrokes to be squandered in service of story and your deepening understanding of it. Every word, every page, every false start, every misstep, every ill-conceived notion, every dead end, every dud joke, every balled-up crumpled piece of paper lying by the waste basket (another missed shot), *everything* between the initial idea and the mailed manuscript is bridge. Just bridge.

We get so hooked on style in so the wrong places. Prize clarity instead. Seek information instead. If you treat your development documents as disposable items, you'll be usefully less precious about them. Neatness doesn't count. Style doesn't count. Clarity counts. Information counts.

Since its only goal is discovery, bridge writing gives you the sloppy liberty you need to try out ideas on the page. That's where they contend. On the page. That's where they start to grow.

premise pages

Some writers go from a one-paragraph story directly to story outline. Call me a development fetishist (some have), but I prefer the interim step of premise pages because they yield maximum information for minimum effort. I'll show you what I mean in a moment, but first write a fresh one-paragraph story, just to remind yourself what that looks like.

> *A lethal viral agent is stolen, and only super sleuth CAROL McCOY can stop a deadly outbreak. With help from her sidekick, KIM LIN, Carol uncovers a NEO-DARWINIST CONSPIRACY to cull the human herd. Using her patented cleverness and grit, Carol defeats the conspiracy, but knows that she's only cut off one of the hydra's many heads.*

Keep rewriting your paragraph until you understand it as well as one paragraph permits. Then take it to this next level: Write a document that runs two or three pages in length—no more—and tells the story as fully as two or three pages will allow.

Here's the first paragraph from premise pages for the opening moments of a soupy family drama on TV.

16-year-old LARINA comes home from the orthodontist with new braces on her teeth. Her mom, SUE, assures her that she looks fine. Larina tries to sell it to herself in the mirror, and she's almost there when BRAD, her kid brother, arrives and mocks her appearance. Larina sags. This is gonna be bad.

Write the first paragraph of premise pages for something.

Write your premise pages as a simple, declarative, present-tense telling of your tale—and now more than ever don't get bogged down in detail. A tough limit on your page count helps with this; in fact, that's why it's there. When you're trying to boil a big story, maybe even an epic, down to (at most) three pages (okay, single-spaced), you'll find that real information crowds out extraneous detail in your words' own Darwinian war to make it to the final draft.

Misguided words, they still don't get it. They don't get to make it to the final anything. After you've done several drafts of your premise pages, you're just going to move on to outline anyhow, leaving all the beautiful words of the premise pages behind. Misguided words, they shouldn't fall so in love with themselves.

Which is not to say that you don't need details. But think in terms of *key details*. At this stage of development, for example, you may need to know if your story involves guns, but you don't need to know what brand.

The following types of detail make useful contributions to premise pages:

- actions

    Randy finds Kate in bed with another man.

- characteristics

    Owen is a fast-talker.

- intentions

    Billy wants to quit his job.

- emotions

    Clarissa feels joy.

- revelations

    Carter realizes that Maxim can't be the killer.

- relationships

    Kris and B.B. love one another.

- events

    The bus goes over a cliff.

- surprises

    Gloria discovers she's pregnant.

- lessons

    Larina comes to love her new look.

- backstory

    Vaughan hasn't seen his sister since the war.

Yes there's some overlap. A bus going over a cliff is not just an event but also an action, and no doubt quite a surprise. The labels don't matter; all that matters is keeping the information useful.

Here are some types of detail that just clog your premise pages:

- literary pretension

  The light breaks but softly, through yonder Juliet-shaped window.

- analogy

  Montgomery paces the room like a nervous cat in a room full of other nervous cats.

- opinion

  We meet Grover. He could stand to lose a few pounds. In fact more than a few. In fact, he's a real Hefty Bag.

- tangents

  The young vagabonds cross Trafalgar Square, which was built to commemorate Lord Nelson's sea victory against Spain in 1805.

- pounds of nouns

  The room is littered with old newspapers and magazines, pizza boxes, beer cans, soda cans, junk mail, video tapes, compact discs and even more litter than that.

- stylishness

Clarissa floats through world civilization class, a cloud-nine passenger now that Bobby has declared his megatonic love for her at last.

Restrict your writing to hard information. It's not glamorous, but, again, it isn't meant to be. To get free from the need for style or pretension in these pages, consider that you're just recording data and storing it on the page for later playback.

Still, writing such chuffa can be fun, so write some now, to get a feel for the difference between meaningful detail and extraneous waste.

Premise pages containing the right sort of information come across as lean, spare, and fast-paced. Bogged down in verbiage or extranea, they become lumbering difficulties: hard to read, hard to edit, and hard to use for development.

Everything in your premise pages should advance your story. Anything that's just there for texture or mood is immediately suspect and can probably profitably be cut.

But the first time through, just go nuts. Write your premise pages as fast as you can. Don't rewrite as you go. Get to the end first, and then go back. Use simple, powerful, clear language. Overwrite but don't embellish. That is, record everything that comes to your mind in sufficient detail to work with it later, but not in so much detail that you get bogged down or stop. Stay within the page count! As you encounter story problems—dead ends, interest drops, or irreducible plot conflicts—don't worry about solving them now. Write around them or push past them. Live with stupid solutions. A stupid solution is all you need for now.

To get a quick fix on how premise pages work, even before you write new ones, try taking a story you're already done with and boiling it back down into this form. Try it especially with a story that never quite worked for you, and get a revealing new look at why that happened.

Or, you know, put something fresh on its feet.

But do put *something* on its feet at this time; the benefit dwells in your words, not mine.

As you rewrite your premise pages, the story starts to take shape—not so much polished (since polish isn't the aim here) as sorted out. You sift and choose among alternatives, and an organic, coherent yarn begins to emerge. Thanks to page limits and plain language, your creative task is well under control, and you quickly become comfortable making big story changes on this small scale.

How many drafts of the premise pages should you do? The unequivocal answer is . . . it depends. Sometimes you get most of the heavy lifting done on the first pass. Other times you go ten rounds with a story and never quite pin it. In any event, you'll be more willing to tackle the next draft, whether it's your second, seventh or 17th, if you've kept the page count down. It's just mentally easier to accept the challenge of rewriting only three pages. And that's the secret to success with premise pages. They let you do conscientious, rigorous, useful development work, there on the page, without being crushed by the sheer volume of words.

In premise pages you're never far from done with a draft.

It's *preciousness* you want to avoid. The more you detach from the need for "quality presentation" in these works, the more ably you can concentrate on cracking the story. Here's a sample hunk from premise pages for act one of a one-hour TV detective show. Note how appropriately approximate the details are at this level. For instance, we know that someone is murdered at the start of the story, but we don't yet know who or how.

> *Someone rich is robbed and brutally murdered. JOE DONNER investigates. He finds evidence at the scene that points to one HECTOR LOPEZ. Lopez is Donner's former best friend, a high-class cat burglar who could never play by any rules but his own. Donner and Lopez fell out years ago over Lopez's attitude.*
>
> *Years later, Donner busted Lopez in a burglary that went wrong, thanks to Lopez's partner, an arrogant and sloppy—but violent and deadly—crook named DAN GALT. Lopez served his time. Now he's a security consultant, currently working for a new museum.*

> *Donner and the museum's head of secu-*
> *rity, GINA THOMASIAN, who clearly*
> *doesn't trust Lopez, question Lopez. Lopez*
> *insists that he's gone straight and knows*
> *nothing about the murder.*
>
> *Later, though, Lopez calls Galt, and warns*
> *him to back off. Galt says he'll be happy*
> *to—when Lopez agrees to cooperate in*
> *Galt's scheme. Lopez tells Galt to go to*
> *hell. Meanwhile, Donner decides to give*
> *Lopez the benefit of the doubt—people do*
> *change, after all.*
>
> *Then a second robbery/murder takes*
> *place. The killer is Dan Galt, but the*
> *evidence he plants at the scene undeniably*
> *fingers Lopez. Reluctantly, Donner puts his*
> *one-time friend under arrest.*

Appropriate level of detail: We know that Lopez con-
tacts Galt; we don't know where or how. We know that
a second murder takes place; we don't know where or
how. With premise pages, it's okay not to know. Move
from the general to the specific, yeah, but how do you
make that move if you don't write the general first?

Also . . . I'm not perfect. As I reread my material, this
phrase just jumps off the page at me:

> *a high-class cat burglar who could never*
> *play by any rules but his own*

And it pisses me off. It is cliché, editorial nonsense,
and I want to cut it out. No, honestly, I want to *destroy it!*

But I'll just leave it there, because it demonstrates two conflicting rules of premise pages. On one hand, I want to be precise and authentic and drive the story forward. On the other hand, I want to *not-edit* as I go. How do I reconcile this conflict?

First write, then rewrite. Move draft by draft toward precision and authenticity, but don't worry if you're not yet there. By the time you get to the end of the whole development process, your premise pages will be so much yesterday's news that you'll wonder why you ever sweated a single choice.

No matter what you're writing—crime drama or caper comedy or stories of the human heart or whatever— you're basically confronting this mystery: *What happens next?* Premise pages allow you to speculate on that question, to pose possible answers, to *explore,* without over-investing.

If you haven't already done so, write premise pages for a story you'd like to develop. Don't worry about the mess, but also don't stop till you reach the end. Remember, it's only three pages away.

Now rewrite for clarity. Start to resolve the story problems that present themselves. Try different solutions. When you get stuck, just stop and gather more information. If you encounter several likely paths through a section of your story, and you can't decide which way to go, do this: *Decide anyhow!* It's an arbitrary choice and one you can always change later.

Keep rewriting until your story starts coming together. And it will come together, so long as you stay flexible, keep your page count down, and constantly make room for new ideas. As the drafts progress, you'll find that the size of the changes you make becomes smaller. You'll come to know your story as well as this level of detail allows.

Here are two strategies for rewriting. Both work, and each has its own utility. Try both to discover which works best for you.

INCREMENTAL REWRITE: Create a new document file and paste your old premise pages into it. Then open up some blank space after each paragraph, rewrite each paragraph in turn, delete the old one and move on. Don't worry about deleting something you might later want. You can always go back and fetch it from the old file. But a policy of *aggressive deletion* will keep your material dynamic and fresh.

UNITARY REWRITE. Print out your premise pages and place them on your desk—face down. Then open a new file and rewrite the premise pages from scratch. An interesting thing happens: Your strongest ideas make it to the next draft intact, and your weakest ideas fall away. This strategy also keeps your story growing, by demanding that your ideas *actively compete* for a home in the next draft.

Keep rewriting until you reach the rewrite that no longer significantly changes your story but just fiddles around with the prose. That will be your cue that it's time to move on. By then, you'll have a document that served this purpose: It took everything you knew about a story in one paragraph and turned it into everything you know about the story in three pages. You've built a platform on which you can stand to reach the next level.

The writer reads the premise pages one last time. She understands her story completely at this level. Never having been here before she didn't know what to expect, but now she feels satisfied. She's ready to tackle the outline.

outline

At this next level of development, we're going to write a story outline. Not this kind of outline:

```
I. AN OUTLINE
   1. That Breaks Everything Down
         a. into tidy indents
         b. and dribbles of data
```

But this kind of outline: A document that tells your tale as fully as possible, in present-tense prose and paragraph form.

I call it an outline, but you could call it a synopsis or a treatment or three other things. The labels don't matter, only the function matters, and that's this: To provide a bridge between the premise pages you just wrote and the script or manuscript you'll soon write.

To write an outline, just take the information present in your premise pages and, remembering to keep your language plain and direct, expand it to the next level of detail. It's at this point that you start to speculate on what kind of gun was used or how, exactly, Larissa's braces make her look.

It's easier to inflate than create. That's why we take the time to develop stories in stages. Rather than invent what we need, whole and complete in the instant, we reinvent what we already have, expanding it a level at a time and a comfortable chunk at a time. It's a relaxed and manageable approach to a writing task that can seem horribly huge and arguably insanely unmanageable.

Here's a paragraph from some premise pages.

> *AUDREY is convinced that no one will ask her to the prom. But she's desperate to go to this defining moment of her adolescence, so she sets out to reinvent herself in some other image.*

Here's how just the first sentence inflates into a paragraph of story outline.

> *AUDREY TURNBUCKLE hates her name. She thinks it's just like the rest of her— ugly and stupid and useless. No wonder no one has asked her to the prom. Who'd want to go with a turnbuckle? Every day she dresses in a futile morning ritual of trying to gild the lily. But today is going to be different. Today Audrey is going to get a new name.*

Obviously I could expand that same starting point in a number of different directions. At this point, as in the premise pages stage, I don't have to commit, but merely explore. Try it. Take the first sentence of your premise pages and inflate it a couple of different ways.

Take the same approach to outline that you took to premise pages. Seek clarity. Be bold and evocative in your language, but don't get bogged down in stylings. Write the first draft as quickly as possible; write it wrong, then start to rework it. Let early drafts serve as bridges to later drafts. Use your outline to deepen your understanding of the mechanics and meaning of the story you've chosen to tell.

At this level of detail, all information is appropriate. The story outline will later serve as the dictionary and encyclopedia for your script or manuscript, so cram it full of data. Just keep it useful and keep it moving. Since an outline is bridge writing, it doesn't have to be pretty but it must be informative and clear. Don't worry if details or story elements conflict at first. With time, and rewriting, the conflicts resolve. It happened with your premise pages and it will happen with your outline too.

How long is an outline? No set limit. Let it be as long as it is. Write till you're done.

Then start over, because rewriting is the key to success with this event. Keep reconsidering your story in light of new information—and keep pumping new information into it. Make changes for substance, not style, but keep making changes. When you get on a good outline roll you may even think that forces are at work beyond your control, but that's just creativity operating in an information-rich environment. Alternatively, if you invoke closure too soon, you'll be stuck with untested choices, and those choices will test your faith. Remember your ultimate goal: a clean, interesting telling of a tale. Not necessarily the tale you started with, nor even, necessarily, the one you intended to tell.

Some writers think that thinking and writing are the same. I don't have that experience. For me to deepen my understanding of a story, I must physically engage in the act of writing it and then writing it again. I really have to put words down on paper.

Those expendable words.

On that recyclable paper.

Why should this be a problem?

Because words take time, and pages take effort, and we want to get it right right now. We'll have to get over that. Invest in your story. Keep learning from it until you know it so well you can't learn anything else at this level of development.

Or until you pull the plug.

That happens too. Stories die in outline. Sometimes you write yourself into a corner; sometimes you lose interest; sometimes you just give up. It's okay. Remember, everything you write, win or lose, adds to your body of work, and that's always a win. Words accumulate; they don't go to waste.

But what a lot of darkness! First the blank page. Then when the pages are no longer blank, they're horrible. They add up (in early drafts) to a story that's forced and plastic and ill-conceived and internally inconsistent and troubled and boring and dishonest and vague. It's hard to keep faith during this phase. But if you do—if you just keep rethinking and rewriting the thing until what's forced and plastic falls away—you'll end up with a sturdy, well-tested document you can trust. A blueprint for what you write next.

'script

Script and manuscript differ at least in this: Scripts are meant to be performed, and manuscripts are meant to be read. Also, scripts have to obey more—and more specific—rules of form. For these and other reasons, you confront different choices in writing screenplays or stage plays or teleplays from those you confront in writing novels, short stories or other forms of print narrative. For ease of use, we'll take the contraction *'script* to represent this end stage of development, the pretty part, the part you try to sell.

'Script differs from story in that it no longer addresses the question of "what happens next?" That question should have been thoroughly explored and sufficiently answered in outline. (If yes, continue; if no . . .) Now style matters. Now we're ready to seek deftness and elegance and even (so we dare hope) eloquence. The tree is up; it's time to hang the tinsel.

If you go to 'script with a good strong outline, you get to write with confidence. Your mystery novel or kid fiction or romantic comedy or spec episode of *She's Deeply Confused* moves forward under control, safe in the cradle of structure. That's a 'script you can write. That's a task you can handle.

Which is not to say that you absolutely must have an outline and absolutely can't write intelligibly without one. Rejecting absolutes absolutely like I do, I'd be the last guy in this book to make that claim. I just know from experience that a 'script started without an outline is not a favorite to finish. There are simply too many questions and not enough answers on the naked page. Suppose I started my novel like this:

```
CHAPTER ONE: THE BEGINNING

  Pearl stood at the top of the steps
leading down into the subway. She
thought of all the times she'd gone
down these steps, or come up them,
tired and spent after another long day
delivering on some idiot's whims. She
sighed hugely and started down. "Hope
I have exact change," she thought.
```

If that's all the information I have, I'm toast. I can't grow finished fiction from this. Right away I have to make story choices that I don't trust—*can't* trust—because I haven't lived with them or studied and examined them yet. But if I'm using a well-worked outline as my foundation, I know where to go next.

Working from an outline, we find that the act of writing is again not so much an act of creation as one of translation. We started with a one-paragraph story and translated it into premise pages. Then we translated premise pages into outline. Now we're translating outline into 'script. We're building on what's there, and not thin air. Though I reject absolutes absolutely, it absolutely makes a difference.

> *So hooray for outline. But now I'm in 'script. I don't want just to tell the story in a more detailed way—I want the thing to come alive. How can I make that happen?*

Good question. Here are some answers.

use prisms

If you're having trouble bringing a moment to life, stop to consider the expectations of the characters locked in the moment. Explore what they want to happen next, and simply convey that desire on the page.

A guy just got out of prison. Make his expectations come to life in prose.

A husband and wife meet in a lawyer's office to discuss their divorce decree. Write their expectations in dialogue form.

Now apply the same principle to something you've been working on. Don't worry about whether this new writing fits in with the old. Just experience what it's like to focus your thoughts through the prism of expectation.

All characters have expectations. They also have fears, urges, addictions, habits, denials, passions and purpose. You can write through these prisms too, with each prism offering a wholly different way to address your scene.

Assign a character a habit, then manifest that habit in a moment of 'script.

→

Again, don't expect to get it right on the first try, and don't fret if you don't. 'Script writing is rewriting too. You create and investigate alternative approaches to a chapter or a scene and, thus armed with comprehensive information, go back and choose from among your contenders.

stay new

Challenge yourself to express your ideas and images in ways they haven't been expressed before. (To quote an old saying, "avoid clichès like the plague.") This is a challenge for sure. We all use the same language. With a few exceptions, we all have the same words to choose from. But in that sense, painters only have the variations of three colors—red, green, blue—to choose from. Yet, somehow, some artists use those three colors to lift their work above the level of cliché. Same with pop songs. Popular songwriters all work with the same limited set of major and minor chords, but the music they make with these same old chords often comes out sounding astoundingly fresh and new. This is a function either of original vision or sheer stubbornness, and even if you feel you don't have vision, you can always invoke stubbornness. Refuse to let your work dwell in the typical.

Try this fun thing. Take something you wrote a *long time* ago and edit it for clichès. Just take a pen and circle everything that's tired or hackneyed or derivative in your dialogue or prose. Then be smug about how far you've come since then.

Clichès live not just in language but in also in actions, interactions, behaviors, feelings, emotions, hopes, dreams and story choices. You have the tools to rise above cliché. But check yourself now and ask whether you have the *willingness* to rise above cliché. It's not easy. It demands rethinking almost everything you write, and testing it against a rigorously high standard. But let's face it, work that stands out *stands out*. If that's what you want of your work, you're going to have to work to get it.

delve

Whenever I recruit writers for training, I look for a quality of *genuineness* in their work. I want the writers with the smallest gap between who they are and who they present themselves to be. To be the sort of writer who gets work, just spend all your time being the sort of writer you are.

In other words, be honest.

Be honest on the page.

Delve. Look for the intersection between your skills and your awareness. In that place, you'll find the writing is usually fresh and new because it's so totally you. Nobody else gets to have your thoughts. They just don't. That's what makes yours so useful to you. Writers excel as a function of their willingness to reveal.

Try this: Write a page or a scene of something that you would never, ever show to anyone else. Write the most horrible, despicable, awful depraved utterings you can imagine. Know that this is your hidden secret. No one will ever see it.

Now show it to someone.

Did you die? Did you lose their approval because you told a dark secret? To the contrary, you likely earned their admiration for being able to confront and express what the rest of us feel and keep hidden. So much of writing is editing, and so much of editing is *"I can't say that. I'll never get away with that."* But to keep your 'script bright and alive and original and crisp, you *must* say what you *can't* say.

Delve. Present your deepest emotions, feelings and fears on the page. Seek the emotional core of the moment, where you feel that your narrator or character is at least speaking the truth. When you see a character lying or prevaricating or denying, talking around the issue rather than confronting it, that's the place to delve.

Go back and examine something you've written. Take the half-truths and make them whole-truths instead.

When you write the whole truth you reap the unexpected benefit of mental repose. Why? Because the half-truth creates a conflict between what you're writing and what you *wish* you'd written. Write the truth, and this conflict goes away. You feel more relaxed, at peace and confident. Simply by telling the truth.

paint

One difference between prose and script is that narrative fiction can *say* what a script must *show*. If a character in a movie or teleplay or stage play has a given emotion, the writer must convey that emotion through the character's actions or words. He can't just say, "You can tell by her face that she's thinking of France." In prose, the author has the luxury of directly expressing the character's thoughts. In both cases, though, you can make the scene or setting come alive by painting the place with original description. Again, the challenge is to go beyond cliché, and present the *place* of the action as some place unique in all the worlds of all writers' imaginings.

Describe the setting for discovery of pirates' gold.

Did you go to a desert island or an underwater shipwreck? Or did you decide to find treasure in a place it's not usually found?

>   *Imagine Father Tom's surprise when he*
>   *found gold dubloons in the collection plate.*

Painting becomes easier when you move away from the typical, but wherever you go, remember to go there with all your senses. How cold or hot is your setting? What does it smell like? Is there dust? Noise? Can you populate the background with passers-by? Closely examine your scenes to make them come to life.

Write a scene in script form, then write it again in prose.

Now write a scene in prose form, then write it again in script.

Note what is appropriate to each form. Note also the discoveries that you make in one form that you miss in the other. I use this trick sometimes when I'm having trouble setting a scene in a script. I know that prose offers me a freedom that script does not allow, so I use that freedom—I write the prose—to explore the scene more fully. Then I take my discoveries back to the script. This is allowed. All it costs is time. Be the sort of writer who is willing to trade time and exploration for quality gains.

ghost logic

I wrote a script about a woman who inherits her father's boat, and also her father's ghost. A friend read it and told me that I had violated the "rules of ghost logic." I didn't get it. How could ghosts have logic when the whole thing was fantasy to begin with? It was, he explained, a matter of consistency. Ghosts can follow any rules you choose to invent, but those rules have to be consistently applied. Early in my story, ghosts could walk through walls, but later, at the climax, they suddenly couldn't do it. For the sake of story convenience I had violated story consistency— and the rules of ghost logic.

Don't confuse *consistent* with *repetitive*. But do be aware that your material makes certain promises to the reader, and one strong promise you make is that you won't arbitrarily change the rules. If you've established a serious tone, say, and then suddenly throw in some slapstick, your reader or audience will likely feel betrayed.

For the sake of buying into your reality, readers and audiences will grant you incredible license. They'll accept pretty much any set of rules you care to impose on the world of your story, so long as you declare your rules—*ghosts exist, but cannot walk through walls*—and stay true to your rules throughout. But arbitrarily changing the rules on your readers feels like cheating to them, and they usually won't put up with it.

Tone, style, language choices, dialogue choices, levels of awareness . . . all of these aspects of your work require consistent presentation. Once you're aware that consistency is an issue, it becomes an easy matter to deal with. Simply police your writing with the yes/no inspection we've already learned to use. *Is this section consistent with the others? If yes, continue; if no, fix.*

There are always two ways to fix the problem of inconsistency. One is to eradicate the inconsistency, but the other is to go back and change the rules. Your audience will accept whatever you need them to accept, *even consistent inconsistency,* if you just give them the news up front.

Go back and examine something you've written recently. Spot, and fix, inconsistencies of tone, voice, language, etc.

To keep your characters consistent, just endow them with powerful and unique filters. They will say and do things in a consistent manner because they are operating under controlling ideas and primary orientations which cover them and drive their actions. If you find that your characters are *not* behaving consistently, go back and examine their filters. It may be that the things which control your characters are not yet completely clear to you.

If you fear that you'll be constantly looking over your own shoulder to test for consistency, don't worry. Over time, the rules of ghost logic become ingrained. That is, you become aware of where you're being inconsistent as you write. Soon, consistency becomes second nature. You test automatically as you type.

break rules

I once wrote copy for recruitment ads, trying to persuade dull-minded engineers to swap their pre-existing form of soul-killing wage slavery for a newer, bigger, better one. Conscripted into this service for the princely sum of $165 a week, I felt like a big shot because I was *writing* for a living. In my (predictably) brief tenure on the job, I wrote endless variations on "Get the Best of Both Worlds," "Challenge Yourself—Reward Yourself," and the deathless, "You Know the Rules, Now Break Them." The fiction they were selling (okay, *I* was selling) was that things would be better for you, you sad techno-dweeb, if you worked *here* instead of *there*.

But it's a funny thing about "you know the rules, now break them." I kind of believe it works. I've seen tons of material (as have you) that succeeds despite the rules. Movies with unruly structure. Novels with stinky punctuation. Short stories with vile usage. What gives? How come some writers (asked Quentin Tarantino of e e cummings) seem to get away with *anything?*

Answer: moxie. If you're going to break the rules, *break* 'em. If you're going to make sketchy choices, make *bold* sketchy choices. If you choose to offend, *really* offend. If you wish to twist syntax, twistingly do it really. If you want to commit apostrophe catastrophe's, by all mean's be my guest.

But be ready to take the heat.

Because the casual or ungenerous reader will immediately wonder whether you know what you're doing. And if she thinks you *don't* know what you're doing, she'll imagine that you're ignorant or arrogant or both, and disconnect from your work. Also consider the possibility that giving yourself license to break the rules might really be just a dodge to avoid facing your own work squarely and judging it honestly.

If you know the rules, you can break them. If you break them and remake them successfully, then you and your readers are in for a treat: a voyage of discovery into new ideas, new ways of presenting those ideas, and new manipulations of the codes that transmit those ideas.

Take some rules and break them. What does that prose or script-stuff look like?

No one says you have to use accepted spelling.
No one says you have to use complete sentences.
No one says you have to be fucking polite.
But you'd better be in control.

Attack your 'script with all the boldness you can muster. Break any rules you choose to break, but be sure you know them first. If you're not sure, *find out*. In all events, let your finished product demonstrate active confidence in itself. Confidence alone covers a multitude of sins.

summary

Okay, so that's development, the slow and steady growth of an idea from inception through interim stages to final form. Some key things to remember:

- *Embrace bridge writing.* Let each draft serve its correct function as a platform for the next.
- *Develop incrementally.* Allow yourself to know the story as well as a given level of detail allows before pushing on to the next.
- *Rewrite ferociously.* The more drafts you do at any stage of development, the fewer problems you'll have at the next.
- *Increase honesty.* Seek a truthful story truthfully told, and keep working at it until it is.
- *Defer closure.* Make the latest possible decision based on the best available information. Let your material live and grow as long as possible before you call it done.
- *Choose boldly.* And then show confidence in the choices you've made.

Development can't be rushed. Stories grow in their own way and at their own pace. It's hard to stay patient when you feel like you're falling behind in your existence, but rushed development only leads to underdeveloped work. What looks like a shortcut is more often a straight shot to a dead end. So be patient with yourself if you can, and allow your projects the crucial time, attention and labor that proper development demands. You'll have the satisfaction, at least, of knowing that you've done your work in a conscientious and orderly way, according to your own high standards.

How to

how to write like the buddha

how to invent new words

how to write a sonnet

how to structure an hour drama

how to generate story ideas
(for episodic television)

how to write like the buddha

The Noble Eightfold Path is a bedrock of Buddhist thought, one of the most sublime prescriptions for living ever written. Intending no disrespect—beyond the disrespect inherent in reducing complex concepts to trivial one-liners—I deconstruct it as follows:

> *RIGHT KNOWLEDGE: Know what life is about.*

> *RIGHT ASPIRATION: Devote yourself to the Path.*

> *RIGHT SPEECH: Say what you mean.*

> *RIGHT BEHAVIOR. Consider your actions.*

> *RIGHT LIVELIHOOD: Work for well-being, not for money.*

> *RIGHT EFFORT: Train the will.*

> *RIGHT MINDFULNESS: Think things through.*

> *RIGHT CONCENTRATION: Enter Nirvana.*

Intending no disrespect—beyond the disrespect inherent in monkeying around with sublime life prescriptions—I was just wondering how the Noble Eightfold

Path would work as a writing tool. Intending no disrespect, I decided to find out.

write knowledge

Write what you know.

But broaden the definition of what you know.

Think beyond where you grew up or where you live now. Your emotions and beliefs, feelings, your observations about life, your points of view and filters, these things are also what you know—and these things make your writing special. To the extent that you know yourself, write yourself. To the extent that you wish to improve your writing, improve your self-knowledge. But world-knowledge counts too, especially if it's data or information that most other writers don't possess. If you're an avid hang glider, your hang-gliding experience gives you unusual insights, a specialized vocabulary, a built-in market for your work, and an interesting story to tell. If you know a great deal about banana slugs, that's kind of gross, but it gives you a leg up on other writers who know less in the highly competitive field of banana-slug writing.

Use your unique experiences to inform your work. Own your knowledge. Invest the events of your life in your work. What unusual work have you done? What are your passions? What do you do for fun? What odd relationships have you had? What quirky people do you know? What subjects do you know quite a lot about?

write aspiration

There is a gap. It's a given. There's a gap between where we are as writers and where we want to be. Worse, no sooner do we reach one level of achievement than we start yearning for the next. So the gap is always shifting, advancing, dancing away from us as our aspirations change. This is frustrating, obviously, and frustration turns to heartache when we contemplate the gap between what we hoped to achieve and what we've been able to achieve so far.

So the question is, how can we address the gap effectively? How can we make frustration go away? One strategy is just *embrace it.* Set out, as your writing job, to *advance the gap.* Just try to write something bigger or tougher or truer this time than last.

Feel yourself grow as a writer. Give yourself the satisfaction of hitting harder targets. This has to do with setting appropriate goals. Here's one I've heard mentioned: *Be a better writer on the day you die than on any other day you lived.* This acknowledges the gap, and acknowledges that the gap will never ever close, which makes the gap easier to accept.

How are you a better writer now than you were last week? What steps are you taking now to be a better writer next week?

write speech

Writing is code. When you write, you encode your thoughts as words on the page. When readers read, they decode your words back into thought. In this sense,

writing and reading resemble the kids' game of telephone, where a whispered phrase is passed down the
line, so that what started out as "hard choices confront
diligent writers" turns into "head cheese converts disco
fever."

What you intend may or may not end up being what
the reader understands. Your task of encoding is easy
when your goal is only to inform, for then you can use
a simple, agreeable code: *Insert tab A into slot B.* But
when the intent is to entertain or persuade or impress
or powerfully move, the code must become more subtle.
This is why clichés are so unhelpful to writers: They convey Thought McNuggets, and not original thought.

In all events, take care with your code and understand its innate authority. Write "Oh bother!" and you're
A. A. Milne. Write *Mein Kampf* and you're Adolph Hitler.
Your words—your codes—have the power to persuade.
And the more you improve as a writer, the greater this
power becomes. So have a care with your choices. Writing is a big stick; watch how you swing it.

What's your most dangerous thought?

write behavior

How do you approach your writer's life? Are you a
serious-minded writer, with a serious practice of writing?
Or are you a "cocktail party writer," the kind of writer
who talks about all the writing he's doing, without actually writing much at all? In truth, we're all somewhat less
serious-minded than we desire, but also significantly less
frivolous than we fear.

Monitor your behavior. Study your writer's life to discover where, when and how you are effective, and where, when and how you slack. Without judging or condemning, set yourself the simple goal of moving toward *greater effectiveness*. Without judging or condemning, liberate an extra half an hour from each day's 24, and dedicate that time to writing. If you find this difficult to do, reflect on the reasons why. Is your day genuinely too clogged, or might you be invoking artificial time pressures to cloak deeper issues of procrastination and fear? Here's a secret: The mere act of thinking about issues like this—not even writing, just *thinking*—will make you a more serious-minded and effective writer over time.

Real writers make real sacrifices. They get up earlier than they'd like, or stay up later than they'd like, if it happens that early and late are the only times they can find the peace and quiet to write. They devote vacations to writing, in service of the day when writing becomes the vocation, not the vacation. They seize random minutes and quarter-hours when minutes and quarter-hours are all they can get. They imagine—and work toward—the perfect writing day that lies ahead, where writing is the only task at hand.

What would your perfect writing day look like? How can you move toward that day?

write livelihood

It's hard to fit a productive writer's life into the corners of your time. It's especially hard to be a working writer at the end of a long day spent at some other task or job. That's why so many writers come home from work and—deservedly, deservedly—crash out on the couch. How do you summon the mental muscle for writing when you've already spent most of the day's available mind on making the nut? It's an obstinate problem, and one that (short of a major lottery win or the death of a rich relative) does not solve itself overnight. But you can take steps. Seek freelance opportunities. Gravitate toward jobs which involve writing—any kind of writing at all. No matter how chumpchange the paycheck, this work will be at least in harmony with, and not at odds with, your long-term writing goals. And this is exactly the sort of work that will move you by degrees of experience and enhanced expertise toward the sort of writer's life you want to have.

What writing job can you get right now for little or even no money?

write effort

There's more to writing than just writing. There's reading, study, practice, drive, discipline . . . craftsmanship. Even as you take steps to improve your writing through writing, think about other steps you can take as well. You're taking one now: reading a how-to text. That's useful because books about writing illuminate and refresh the process of writing—which illumination and refreshment all writers need.

There's more to writing than just generating product. There's writing that's intended only to instruct or inform the writer. The exercises in this book fall into that class, as do journal writing, "free" writing, just-for-the-hell-of-it storytelling, and any other writing that engages your drive, focuses your will, and deepens your understanding of your own capabilities. You can easily train your will—but you have to accept the challenge. Do your drills. Allow yourself to believe that writing improves this way.

Assign yourself a daily writing task, and complete the task every day for a week (or, you know, a decade . . . whatever). Experience the satisfaction that comes from having achieved this goal.

write mindfulness

Writers don't write in a vacuum. (If we did, our flesh would explode.) We live within the context of other people. Some are our allies and some are our enemies. That is, some help serve our writing goals, and some, let's be frank, hinder us. Obviously seek to minimize enemies and maximize allies. But consider the consequence of this: To be the sort of writer you truly want to be, you may have to leave some people behind. You basically leave them behind by seeking and accruing more self-awareness. Self-awareness is vital to a writer. It lubricates absolutely every part of the writing process. But it can be threatening, both to writers and to those around them; people who don't want to move into awareness have been known to fight or subvert the efforts of those who do. If you desire a real practice of writing, it may cost you some pre-existing relationships. It may be that these are relationships you're better off without.

What steps can you take to move toward self-awareness? Who is likely to feel threatened by this?

write concentration

Concentration. Whoo-boy. When it's good, it's great. Writers deeply engaged in the act of writing lose all consciousness of bills, disappointments, aches and pains, human conflict, past failures and future longings. Writers deeply engaged in the act of writing enter a realm where nothing matters but the world coming to life beneath their hands. This is the place. This is where writers want to be, and get to stand: lords of their own creation.

Writing is how we get better at writing. But writing is also how we enter nirvana, the lower-case state of bliss where all is forgotten except the act of writing. You know this state; you've been there before. It's when you suddenly look up at the clock and wonder where the last three hours went. It's when you rock back in your chair and laugh at your own written joke or feel the tender pull of your own expressed emotion or the raw power of your own scary descriptives. It's where you cry at your own words. Nirvana. The place we want to be. Surprise, but it's this simple: You get there by going there. Write long enough, and the past and future fall away, leaving only the transcendent *now,* a state of being known to dogs and small children.

Here's a fun one: Write till you enter bliss.

how to invent new words

Who owns the language? Who controls it? Who makes rules for its behavior? This is an easy question to answer when you're in school: The textbook owns the language and the teacher makes the rules. It's easy to answer on the street too. The people own the language, and consensus—*dude!*—is the rule.

But consensus . . . now consensus is a problem. If I decide on my own, for example, to change the word *truck* into the phrase *sloppy joe,* I can have an amusing little language party all on my own, talking about *flatbed sloppy joes* and *quarter ton sloppy joes* and *year-end rebates on all new sloppy joes in stock.* But if I'm walking down the street and I see a blind priest about to step into onrushing traffic, and I shout out "Watch out for that huge speeding sloppy joe!" my warning falls on a blind man's deaf ears because we don't have consensus. Thus is a righteous cleric needlessly snuffed.

Is it a safety issue, then? Are we conservative with language because we want to communicate with maximum efficiency, and we're afraid that if we grant ourselves language license, things will get too messy? Maybe. But within our microcultures, we already do it all the time. Investigate your memory for a moment and you'll see that it's true. What's that cute descriptive word for a member of the opposite sex that you and your friends all use? How did you say "drunk" when you were 17 so your parents wouldn't know? List some other words and phrases that you, inventive person that you are, have invented.

*dumpkin, clownoid, sitcomsultant,
cubehole, flophead, scrunky, singulural,
smokequarium*

To name a thing is to own a thing. I once worked for a senescent TV producer who kept calling me Jack, Jack Vorhaus. After correcting him several times, I gave up and just let him call me Jack. He felt so proprietary about "his" Jack Vorhaus that he kept assigning me scripts. Did I feel shame in surrendering my name? Not really. Calling me Jack made him feel loyal to me, and it helped me achieve my goal of earning a paycheck through the work of writing.

To name a thing is to own a thing. When you make up new words, or move old words into new contexts, when your word choice is an act of creation and not just selection, you take ownership of the language. And language is a writer's clay.

Take some ownership now. Invent some new words. Don't be afraid to be whimsical.

*Motoficial. Abneviate. Tartantastic.
Skironic. Svoid. Depair. Indigot. Fleen.*

Here's me being not afraid to be whimsical: I now declare all words which begin with the letter *m* begin with *mn* instead. Where once we had the moon in May o'er a new mown meadow, we now have the mnoon in Mnay o'er a new mnown mneadow.

But what does it all mnean, Jack?

For one thing, it mneans that I'm suddenly mnuch mnore attentive to mny word choices. It mneans that as a writer I'm seeing language in a different light. It also mneans that I'm outside consensus, which is where an original writer *mnust* be.

Invent new words to invigorate your language, increase your authenticity and boost confidence in your creative self.

Consensus. I gave a lecture in Australia once and spoke of the need to "lay pipe" in a story, by which I meant "insert exposition." But the audience tittered. It turned out that "lay pipe" was Aussie slang for "screw." That's consensus for you. One man's structure tip is another man's smutty joke. I say *fight consensus!* and I hope you agree.

There are many ways to invent new words. For instance, you can boil verbs out of nouns. Just hunt for nouns that don't normally have verb forms and slap on an *-ing. Slat* into *slatting* or *lamp* into *lamping* or . . .

Or try this. Add *-age* to any common verb. *Weed* into *weedage; tank* into *tankage; drink* into *drinkage.* Don't be afraid to be silly. Who said silly was wrong?

I am a spy in the house of language. I take nothing for given. You have heard of these words: proton, neutron, electron. Your basic parts of the atom. Now how about these: photon, lepton, muon? They're subatomic particles, and if you have even a Discovery Channel knowledge of physics, they don't seem strange to your ear. Did you know there are further subatomic particles called sleptons, bosons, gluons, gravitons, gravitinos, and neutrinos?

And that's to say nothing of quarks.

You got your bottom quarks, top quarks, charmed quarks, flavored quarks, strange quarks and super quarks.

I'm not making this stuff up!

But I could, though, I could. I could invent slow quarks, fast quarks, sparky quarks, even happy, grumpy and dopey quarks. I could give you fluons and nuons and how-do-you-do-ons; pardons and hardons too.

I hear they've just decreed all known names for celestial objects obsolete. "Sun" gone, "moon" gone, "galaxy" gone. What can you give me instead?

Hang on, though, hang on. Just because *we* change a name doesn't mean the name has changed. You might have changed *galaxy* to *SimpsonBruckheimer,* but consensus still knows *galaxy* as *galaxy.* You can't go around promiscuously renaming things if reality won't cooperate.

But reality is *so* subjective.

> *If you went to high school in the 1950s,*
> *your science teacher was a skinny guy*

with a skinny tie, horn rim glasses, and 15 minutes in a French cathouse in the waning days of World War II to show for his sexual experience. Intoning in a mono- tone, he informed you that each and every atom in the universe was comprised of some number of protons, electrons and neutrons. The building blocks of nature! He told you this, and told you it was fact!

*If you went to high school in the 1970s, your science teacher was a hairy guy with a paisley tie, wire rim glasses, and five years of be-ins, love-ins, sit-ins and sleep- ins to show for his sexual experience. Speaking through a deep dope torpor, he alerted you that protons, electrons and neutrons were really made of quarks and leptons and gluons. The building blocks of the building blocks of nature! He told you this, and told you it was **fact**!*

*If you went to high school last week, your science teacher was a celibate with an Armani tie, contact lenses, and no sexual experience to speak of. Reciting subatomic poetry, she blithely declared that 90% of the universe is comprised of dark matter that scientists don't really understand at all. She told you this, and told you it was <u>**FACT**</u>!*

What the fact, huh? Facts are subject to change. New information becomes available, old words are assigned to new concepts, and not only does language change, but reality changes too. And not only does reality change, but language changes too!

Today's electronic transaction is tomorrow's *e-commerce* and there's nothing we can do about that. But when we writers alter reality—on the subatomic level of the letter and the word—*we* are in control. In other words, when you take command of language, they throw reality in for free.

It's easy to reshape reality. Just take existing words and assign them new meanings. *Splurge* means splurge, of course—go wild, spend a lot—only now (according to me) it means *male orgasm* too.

And where will these words come from? So many strategies to choose from. Experiment with the arbitrary. Open the phone book. Harvest the Internet. Use the next three words you hear as one (what's a *hearasone?*) Or just wander in the green pastures of your mind.

I now choose to redefine a number of words equal to the number of function keys on my keyboard.

*F1. Crouch = the sound you make
    wadding up a piece of newsprint.*

F2. Vying = mesh fasteners.

F3. Curvature = overwhelmingly tangible.

F4. Alloy = a secret fear.

*F6. Ameliorate = to vanish or disappear,
    like Amelia Earhart.*

F5. Despair = happiness.

F7. Tatter = a way to cook fish.

F8. Consciousness = ducks.

F9. Anthropomorphic = covered with fur and brightly colored.

F10. Condense = imprison.

F11. Component = media consultant.

F12. Sponge = female orgasm.

John, JV, *Jack*, what does it all *mean*? If all your choices are arbitrary, then there's no basis for choosing. Nonsense must logically result.

Nonsense must *logically* result.

Now there's something to think about.

To make your choices less arbitrary, seek a cognitive link between some words as they're currently commonly understood and the new way you intend to use them. That's what happened when *surf* went from the ocean to the Internet, and when *umbilical* replaced *leash* at my local dog park.

You can also use dead slang as a springboard to new words. Dweeb, nerd, wonk: Though only a few years old, these words already seem obsolete, and they'll make your writing sound stale. But you can easily invent new words that mean the same thing. Start by invoking the nerd. Call up a picture of him in your mind. See the pocket protector, the calculator and the heavy spectacles. Now give that picture a name. I call it "spec-head," capturing both the glasses and the quality of being trapped in parameters.

Alternatively, hunt for new letter combinations with similar sounds. *Dweeb, wonk* and *dink* make me think of *weeb, twonk* and *gink.* In this case, the very *shape* of your constructs—their similarity to existing words—conveys the meaning.

Why invent new words? Beyond a writer's solemn responsibility as guardian of a dynamic, living language, it's just plain fun to build a collection. Try adding prefixes . . .

> *paracritical, preordinary, postliteral,*
> *hypopositive, dislogical, cryptocertified,*
> *dianaylsis, unsmarten, pseudosexual,*
> *promanic, antedata, antipractical, inapt,*
> *unzero, illinebriate, microteen,*
> *malanthropic, foreswelling, phenoscript,*
> *megamyth, dephase, ectonothing*

. . . or subtracting them.

> *meditated murder, thetical questions,*
> *hensile toes, scription drugs, victed felons,*
> *straneous material, vailing winds, tremist*
> *groups, vective, vidious, veterate, vigorate,*
> *volve, voke, dignant, pellant, ception,*
> *wilderment*

Or add suffixes.

> *coffeeesque, happyism, vaultive,*
> *lobotomania, hemption, thrillment,*
> *guestable, medievaling, penisy, slickize,*
> *Illinoiser, newcious, jugfully, requirate,*
> *sparkage, hosiary, plushish, pustulian,*
> *repentology*

Or subtract *them*.

> *voluntar, metamorph, technic, technol,*
> *sapph, dement, occupat, biolog, pestic,*
> *murd, jit, ging, relig, loit, quintess, tapest,*
> *vasect, fet, sund*

→

Or just jam everything together.

> *hypocentric, preism, nonive, endodigm,*
> *tritation, omnography, reable, conicrat,*
> *teleful, protivity, philting, egosophy,*
> *paraphile, enderotic, disly, comatory*

→

I could share all sorts of process analysis here, show you how I derived *phenoscript* from pheno as in pheno-barbitol, as in sleep-inducing, as in snoreful screenplays I have read. Or how I grew *penisy* by cross-breeding -y with a list of sexual terms, and y not? The world can always use another word for dickhead. But in the end, it's *your* process that matters, not mine, so watch your process as you go.

Meanwhile, back at inventing new words, you can also exploit typos. When jargon falls short, you get *jargo*, and an intended felony turns into *velony* when the right finger hits the wrong key. You can make mistakies on purpose, just to find found art.

And you say you don't know how to be inventive. I scof. Which is like scoff, only slightly less so.

You can weld words to make new ones. This one's easy.

> *alternagraph, pharmachute, exersystem, falconstriction, dynamitingale*

Why am I doing your work for you? You have a dictionary. You have all the new words you need.

I know earnest people who teach themselves five new words every day. They learn useful words like circumnavigate, spleen, snood, tetracycline and peristalsis.

That's fine as far as it goes, and I applaud them for their ardent self-improvement. But wouldn't it be more *wellroundifying* to invoke the imagination as well? What about *making up* five new words a day? If nothing else, we learn to live outside the norm, which should make us feel more at home in the world of fiction, which is not, by its nature, the norm.

Plus there's this: A character who can invent new words is a handy one to have around. That's one voice, at least, which you can trust to be cliché-free because it makes up everything as it goes along. And a character who has original command of language probably has original command of ideas as well. Also, using new words puts *your* voice into *your* work. That can't be a bad thring.

So take command of your language, just as you take command of your story and characters and theme. They're your words. You own them. All of them. The ones you create, designate or appropriate. Doesn't that make you feel rich now? Doesn't that make you feel like king of the world?

Or at least king of the word.

how to write a sonnet

Some rules, if you break them, you break everything.

It's a rule of sonnets that a sonnet has *exactly 14 lines*. A five-line sonnet isn't a sonnet. Some sonnets have a rhyming scheme of ABAB, CDCD, EFEF, GG. To make sure your sonnet is kosher, just follow that rule. The lines in sonnets are usually written in iambic pentameter—five syllable-pairs, with the stresses just so: pa-POM pa-POM pa-POM pa-POM pa-POM. Mis-pom your POMs and your sonnet ain't on it.

Sonnets have subtler rules also. It's a rule of some sonnets that the ninth line expresses a reversal of attitude, and that the final couplet sums up the sense or intent or thesis of the piece. These are rules you could get away with bending or breaking. You could have a "sloppy" sonnet, where your attitude never changes or your point never gets summed up. The Lord High Commissioner of Sonnets might disdain your effort, but you could still call it a sonnet.

So that's a lot of rules, but actually that could help, because in this case the rules don't confine, they define. The more specific the rules of form become, the more certain you can be that your solution "works," at least in the sense of conforming to the rules.

If a guy says to me, "Write a screenplay," I'm lost. I don't know where to begin. If a guy says to me, "Write a family-oriented western, preferably based on a true story, with no gratuitous sex or violence and a strong female lead," then I'm in there. I do know where to begin. More to the point, I know what the right answer will look like.

So try writing a sonnet, and examine the freedom that comes from working within tight constraints. This seems illogical on its face, but it's not really. If you declare with certainty that the first line and the third line of your poem must rhyme, then that's one less thing you to have to decide as you go. If you know that each line must have a certain pattern or cadence, then you have a simple, effective way of testing the correctness of your work. Either it fits the pattern or it don't. Either it's a sonnet or it ain't. No two vagues about it.

This is so unlike story, which is nothing but vague for most of the stages of its life, coming into settled confidence only at the end of development. That's why it's useful to have strategies for checking your stories as you go. That's why it's useful to have rules. That's why it's useful to write sonnets, even if you never have before.

For ease of use, let's shoot for a schoolbook sonnet of 14 lines, an ABAB, CDCD, EFEF, GG rhyme scheme, iambic pentameter, 9th line pivot, and final couplet sum-up. That's only a five rules; that should be plenty.

SONNET: EXERCISE AT FORTY

I pause, I stop, I startle, pause and start again,
As near and distant sirens herald crime.
I stop. I seethe, impatient with my pen.
And at the wholesale murder of my time.
This is not new; a high school game I played
With other junior Mensas of my kind:
Self-indulgent brickwork neatly laid,

A puzzle posed to occupy the mind.
A puzzle though that pilfers hours whole
From forty-winter me, who in his youth
Would seize the shortest path to reach his goal
And linger not to taste the deeper truth:
A sculptor should not brutalize the stone,
But coax it till the shape inside is shown.

If you're not happy with your outcome, don't sweat it. For the moment, this is problem-solving, not poetry; just a look at rules. That's the great thing about sonnets. They don't have to be art, or even craft, to be correct. They just have to follow the rules.

It's easy to write a sonnet when you disconnect from outcome, and just follow the rules. But it's hard to write a sonnet (or even write anything, or even *do* anything) if you don't know the rules. If you didn't know the rhyming scheme or the stress pattern or the right number of lines, you and a million monkeys could flog a million typewriters for a million years and still not write a sonnet. So that's the argument for the rules: The better you know them, the easier it is to do some stuff. Which holds for sonnets and screenplays and space shuttles and even crossing the street.

So you know what? Try it again.

Following a pattern may not thrill you,
But writing one more poem will not kill you.

Okay next, write a haiku. First find out what one is.

Okay, next, let's say you wanted to write an hour-drama.

What? You say don't write hour dramas?

Hey, you didn't used to write sonnets.

how to structure an hour drama

You may find this hard to believe, but the structure of drama on commercial television is dictated by commercials.

Shock you, did I? It's true. When all prime-time hours had three commercial breaks (on the quarter- and half-hour), all prime-time dramas had four acts. These days, a lot of hour dramas, especially those off-network, have five acts, and if you think that's to accommodate another commercial, then you're just an old cynic. But anyway, if you're interested in writing five-act dramas, here are some shorthands you can use.

run-time

The first and second acts are the longest ones, with the third, fourth and fifth increasingly shorter. The reason for this is *rising tension*. As the action and drama rise toward a climax, the pace accelerates too. Shorter acts accommodate accelerated pace.

You could break up 60 minutes of television into acts of the following lengths:
- ACT ONE   18 minutes
- ACT TWO   12 minutes
- ACT THREE   10 minutes
- ACT FOUR   10 minutes
- ACT FIVE   10 minutes

But that wouldn't take into account the run-time of the commercials (let's not forget why we're here), so your actual run-time looks more like this, more or less:
- ACT ONE   15 minutes

- ACT TWO   11 minutes
- ACT THREE   10 minutes
- ACT FOUR   8 minutes
- ACT FIVE   7 minutes

Don't worry about the exact numbers. As a rough guide, let the first two acts equal half the script, and the last three acts equal the other half. You won't go too far wrong with that. Remember that a page of script equals a minute of film, more or less. If your script is dialogue-heavy, it'll run longer; if it's action-heavy, it'll run shorter.

thumbnail

Structure your TV stories around rising tension. Tension—jeopardy or trouble—peaks at each act break, then levels off at the beginning of each new act. Then it rises again, to a higher level than before, as the next act nears its end.

Suppose you had a show called *Amanda,* and on that show you had a (radical move, this) lead character named Amanda. If her story in this week's episode were, *"I think I'm in love. No, this time I mean it"* then a thumbnail of the acts might look like this:

- end act one: Amanda and her boyfriend break up.
- end act two: Amanda kisses a new boy.
- end act three: Amanda thinks she's in love.
- end act four: Amanda realizes that Mr. Right is Mr. Monster.
- end act five: Amanda is free and alone—and ready to love again.

Think up another story for Amanda, and run her thumbnail act breaks.

Episodic television shows—and this is true for situation comedy as well as hour drama—tell stories that are essentially circular in nature. Characters end up generally back where they began. We have to return them to their original state, more or less, in order to preserve the serial nature of the show. If the characters change too much from week to week, the audience won't know what to expect when they return. In the nature of revisiting old friends, the audience wants very much to know what to expect when they return. So we can give characters in our shows a new understanding about a given subject, but the fundamentals of their situation generally remain unchanged. In short, you can have your characters win or lose a battle, but they cannot lose or win the war, not if you want to have someplace to go next week.

Thus if you have a murder mystery in which the hero solves a new crime each week, he logically starts out each episode without a current crime to solve. In the course of the episode, he gets a case, struggles to solve it, succeeds, and then ends up right back where he started: without a current crime to solve.

Do a couple of thumbnails for a murder mystery involving a cop-and-robot partnership or, alternatively, for a current television show you'd enjoy writing for.

I use a thumbnail strategy in developing dramatic stories for television because I want to be sure, with the minimum investment of time and effort, whether I've got a real beginning, middle, and end to my tale, and whether I have real act-endings, or *act breaks,* to shoot for.

act breaks

Think of your act breaks as cliffhangers, but remember that cliffhangers can be emotional as well as physical. Which is right for your show? It depends on the rules of your show. If it's a "hero-escapes" show, then the act breaks are "hero-is-trapped" breaks. If it's a soap opera, then the act breaks involve rifts in relationships. Many audiences find the most satisfying hour dramas to be ones that force characters to face both physical and emotional risk.

If you have an ensemble cast, you can assign big dramatic moments to different characters at different act breaks. Based on no particular information, I predict that the ensemble cast of *Amanda* is in for troubles like these:

Amanda gets pregnant.
Bernice is in debt.
Ruthie fights with her hyper-controlling parents.
Rob is an adrenaline junkie.
Claudia has a drug problem.
Joe can't find work.
Tonja and Dougie have an affair.
Tonja and Frank have an affair.
Tonja and Leanne have an affair.

(Oh, that Tonja.) Or troubles like these:

Once you have some cardboard-cutout characters and a rough emotional universe, you can look at the cliffhanger structure and lay out some act breaks in usefully simple terms. Suppose we decide that in this episode of *Amanda*, Tonja and Frank get it on, Ruthie confronts her parents, and Rob and Joe buy a jet boat.

THE STORY STARTS: *Tonja asks Frank out.*
Ruthie hears that her parents are coming.
Joe learns of a jet boat for sale.

BREAK ONE: *Tonja and Frank make love.*
Ruthie's parents arrive.
Joe convinces Rob to be his business partner.

BREAK TWO: *Tonja takes another lover.*
Ruthie's parents order her home.
Joe and Rob buy the boat.

BREAK THREE: *Frank discovers Tonja's infidelity.*
Ruthie gives up and goes home.
Joe and Rob discover they've been swindled.

BREAK FOUR: *Frank confronts Tonja.*
Ruthie runs away.
Joe and Rob blame each other and fall out.

BREAK FIVE (end):   *Tonja commits to Frank.*
Ruthie asserts—and wins—her independence.
Joe and Rob kill their partnership but save their friendship.

In just 15 sentences you can acquire the bare bones for an hour's worth of television. Try using this structure to map an episode of *Amanda* or a show you like or one you just made up.

→

Note that each character has cliffhangers—act breaks—for his or her own story. To keep their stories moving in the right direction, just drive them, act by act, to points of higher peril. Remember that each story should reveal your characters in new and interesting ways without changing their fundamental nature. You should be able to ask and answer this question of every character in every story you write (and not just TV tales, in fact): *In what new and interesting way is the character revealed?* And then you should be able to ask of each moment within the story: *How does this moment further that end?*

Act-break moments fall into categories. Two of these include change of state and new information. Buying the jet boat is a change of state; finding out that it's worthless is new information. Other classes of action that drive act breaks include threats introduced, secrets revealed, decisions made and what else?

→

Any class of action works as an act break, so long as it boils down to this: A NEW BIG THING. For the health of your hour drama, put a new big thing at the end of every act. Because the point of all this (did you forget?) is to hold the audience through the commercial break.

> *Is she going to keep the baby? Did he really dodge the draft? How will they get*

> *out of this mess now? Let's stay tuned and find out!*

List some questions that would keep an audience's attention and bring them back after the ads.

trigger and root

In episodic television, there is a direct causal connection between where the problem starts and how the character solves it. We can call this connection *triggering event* and *root action* or, more simply, *trigger and root*. And we can use it to figure out a story by simple deduction. If you know the triggering event *(Ruthie's parents are coming to visit)* you can predict the root action *(she'll stand up to them this time).*

> *Trigger:*   *Inspector Barlett finds a body.*
> *Root:*   *Inspector Barlett nabs the killer.*
>
> *Trigger:*   *Becky tackles a difficult task.*
> *Root:*   *Becky masters the task at last.*
>
> *Trigger:*   *The Bomb Squad gets a suicide mission.*
> *Root:*   *The Bomb Squad pulls it off.*
>
> *Trigger:*   *Banks gets fired from a job.*
> *Root:*   *Banks is happy in his new job.*

Try a few triggers and roots.

This trigger and root strategy applies to other kinds of stories besides episodic drama. Pretty much any time you have a hero, you can map the story in its simplest terms by looking for the connection between the problem that assaults the hero and what the hero ultimately does to solve it.

You can also solve the problem in reverse. If you know the root—*Juno kills the bad guy*—you can backpredict the trigger—*a bad guy threatens Juno*.

> *Root:*   *War is averted.*
> *Trigger:* *War is threatened.*
>
> *Root:*   *Happy moves back home.*
> *Trigger:* *Happy moves away.*
>
> *Root:*   *Amanda goes to the dance.*
> *Trigger:* *Amanda hears about a dance.*

To put trigger and root into context, consider that each act break in your story is somewhere along the road from trigger to root. At the trigger, a problem is postulated. At the root, the problem is solved. In between, the problem becomes larger and the stakes get higher as each act break passes.

trouble

If you're still having trouble nailing your act breaks, think of them in terms of trouble. Here are act breaks translated into trouble.

Break one: trouble is predicted
Break two: trouble is coming
Break three: trouble is here
Break four: trouble is winning
Break five: trouble is gone

Remember the circular nature of television drama. The departure of trouble at the end of act five represents a return to the characters' original state of being.

Here's thrill-seeker Rob encountering *trouble*.

TROUBLE IS PREDICTED: *Rob learns of a dangerous new thrill to seek.*

TROUBLE IS COMING: *Rob decides to try the new thrill.*

TROUBLE IS HERE: *Rob engages in a dangerous act.*

TROUBLE IS WINNING: *A terrible accident threatens Rob's life.*

TROUBLE IS GONE: *Rob gets rescued and moderates his lust for kicks.*

Map a couple of stories in terms of trouble.

In a story with real drive, your character can't get out of trouble without going through it. Once you pull the trigger, there should be no evasion sufficient, nor denial strong enough to keep your character from the ultimate confrontation. Once Rob learns that there's a new death sport out there, he's bound to go try it, and his story won't be finished till he does.

point of attack

If you're having trouble with *trouble,* try challenging your character with a *point of attack.* Do this either by *introducing a desire* or by *removing a need.* If Dougie has a crush on the new girl, that's your point of attack on him. If Claudia's dope supply is cut off, that's your point of attack on her.

Generate some interesting points of attack.

Once you have a point of attack, you're ready to build a story on the now-familiar structure of rising tension, something like this:

Break one:	point of attack
Break two:	anxious suspense
Break three:	authentic threat
Break four:	life-and-death struggle
Break five:	outcome

POINT OF ATTACK: Claudia's dealer gets busted.

ANXIOUS SUSPENSE: She fears to go through withdrawal.

AUTHENTIC THREAT: She buys bad dope from a stranger.

LIFE-AND-DEATH STRUGGLE: She overdoses.

OUTCOME: In doubt.

It's okay to have the outcome in doubt. At this stage of development, you may not know how the story ends, nor do you need to. In hour-drama there are really only three possible outcomes: somebody wins, somebody loses, or the verdict is deferred. If Claudia goes into detox, she wins. If she dies, she loses. If she goes into a coma, the verdict is deferred. But notice that we don't need to know the outcome in order to develop the story to this level.

Write a story using the *point of attack* template.

Can't swing a dead cat around here without hitting a template, huh? But in the end it still comes down to a writer in a room, contemplating options. *Would Rob wear a helmet? What kind of drugs does Claudia use? What's Ruthie's beef with her parents anyhow?* How do we figure these things out? By asking the right kinds of questions. The more precise your questions are, the likelier you are to answer them well.

Once you have your act breaks worked out, consider them telephone poles and make it your job to connect the wires from pole to pole. At this point, you can write premise pages for your hour drama, using the act breaks you've devised. You may find that the task is easier this way because you have so many clear targets to hit.

how to generate story ideas (for episodic television)

Here's are 19 strategies you can use to generate story ideas for episodic TV or almost any other form of fiction. Some of these I made up. Others I, you know, stole.

1. Steal. Obviously you can steal from yourself, from old ideas or half-baked stories that never got off the ground in different circumstances. You can also steal from others simply by putting an old story in a new setting. Sure *Romeo and Juliet* has been done to death, but if it's never been done on your show, then it's fresh and new and useful.

2. Put pairs of characters together and explore their relationships. Remember that everyone has relationships to others, even people they hate. When you need a story, you can always ask, "Where is this relationship now, and where is it going next?"

3. Look for your characters' frailties. If a character is tedious, attack his pedantic nature. If a character denies her feelings, force her to confront them. The truth is revealed under pressure, so put your characters under pressure to force them to confront these truths.

4. Build story on theme. If your theme is "find love," let your story be a search for love. If your theme is "kill bad guys," don't stop till all the bad guys are dead. Write about themes that are important to you. Attach themes to stories about characters most in need of learning the lesson you wish to teach.

5. Explore aspects of your characters' inner lives. What are their fears, vices, obsessions, hobbies, beliefs

or recreations? These aspects, examined and listed, will provide reliable springboards to story.

6. Seek pain and suffering. Look at what makes your characters ache. Also examine what makes you ache. Emotional sore spots trigger story—if you can stand to face them.

7. Think about your personal struggles in this moment and ask how you can project onto your characters your own feelings, awareness, philosophy, dreams, desires, conflicts, relationships or observations. This sort of story has innate emotional authenticity because it comes from a place within you that's honest and real.

8. Examine first times. First date, first dog, whatever. Impose a change of state on a character's circumstance. When a story begins with the phrase, "for the very first time . . ." it's off to a smart start.

9. Look for the money scene, a scene that you just *know* will be richly rewarding, or drop-dead funny, or scary as hell. Then build a story backward from there. If you can picture a moment in a restaurant where the lying double-daters find each other out and hilarity ensues, use that scene to backpredict the story leading up to it.

10. Find characteristics inappropriate to a character, and assign those characteristics on a temporary basis. If a character is normally quite generous, it's worth exploring the time when she becomes a tightwad. It's easier to build a story around resistance than around accord.

11. Think about themes that are important to your audience. Build stories that illuminate those themes. Everyone is concerned with issues of love, death, health, self-image and so on. Stories built around these core human concerns have a natural appeal to a broad audience.

12. Think about a thing your character could never, ever do or think or say. Then construct the circumstances that demand her to do or think or say that thing.

13. Generate a list of the stupidest, least likely ideas you can imagine. Even if the ideas seem unworkable, they're usually only a change or two away from useful. Even if your character can't actually die, he could *think* he's dying, couldn't he?

14. Think of situations that force your characters to stay together against their will. Trap them in circumstance. For instance, find characters who hate each other's guts and then give them mutual strong sexual attraction or a common interest or a joint business. Or even handcuffs.

15. Explore taboo subjects. Look for stories that are over the edge, then find a way to pull them back. To lessen the impact of taboo, you can always shift it to a less threatening context. But don't shy away from a subject. To the extent that stories are intended to unsettle an audience, story begins where tolerance ends.

16. Think about things you enjoy, or would enjoy writing about, and put them into your stories. For example, if you'd like to write stand-up comedy material, conceive a story where one of your characters develops a comedy act.

17. Exploit your areas of special expertise or knowledge. If you're a chess pro, write a chess tale. If you know cheese, write cheese. For the sake of unique, authentic stories, drag your real-world experience into your work.

18. Come up with interesting, fun or provocative titles first, and then develop stories which deliver on the promise of those titles.

19. Don't forget fantasy.

Writer's Life

been there

conditionals

writing with a partner

writers and editors

practice practice

writer's block

q & a

been there

Here's some e-mail I once got from a struggling writer friend.

> *'98 was a horrible year jobwise. So glad '99 is here. Looking for an hourlong dramatic writing gig if you have any suggestions.*

Been there. Gracious, have I been there. Am there still, in the sense of that senseless optimism. *We writers never give up.* We keep putting nickels in the hope machine—that existential slot machine—and pulling the handle as hard and as fast as we can. We want the jackpot, of course: **BLOCKBUSTER!** or **BROADWAY!** or **BESTSELLER!** But we'll settle for any kind of payout from the hope machine, so long as we get enough back to stay in the game.

We just want to stay in the game.

I have three regular hope machines, ones that I play every day. Each is bright and shiny, and each addicts me completely.

- The currency for my Hollywood hope machine is pitch meetings and premise pages, story outlines and spec scripts. It pays off with script assignments and staff jobs, development deals and blind pilot commitments. The jackpot would be my own show, or maybe a **MAJOR MOTION PICTURE!** starring (dare I hope it?) **SANDY SALTWATER!**

- My literary hope machine feeds on short stories, novels, and how-to books like this. It pays off with excerpt rights, reprint rights, royalty payments and backdoor movie deals. Small jackpots include book tours and favorable press. The big jackpot would be I'm Mark Twain.
- My teaching hope machine consumes guest appearances at writers' conferences, consulting gigs and weeklong workshops in overseas hotels. The jackpot would be a juicy big consultancy, but the small daily payout is the satisfaction of knowing I've helped writers.

It's not unreasonable to have more than one hope machine. Common hope machines include ones for *family, career, wealth* . . .

Writers' hope machines are all about the magical day when *wanting to be a writer* has turned into *am a writer*.

So visualize one of your hope machines. Imagine it's a slot machine. See the coin-drop slot and the handle you have to (get to) pull. Take a good close look at the reels. What symbols spin on the slot machine of your dreams? What payouts do you yearn for? Which ones will you settle for? What would your jackpot be? Be honest in your descriptions; there's no one in this casino but you.

Okay, so hope. We know all about hope. We have all the hope machines we need, and not one of the damn bandits is paying out like we'd like it to. Where do we get some patience? What aisle do they sell that in?

If your goal is to improve as a writer, you're a lock to succeed, and it's easy to be patient. If your target is screenplay superstardom or selling that novel, your odds are much longer, and you know you'll have to grind it out over time. Perhaps awareness of the grind will give you the patience you need. But what if the odds seem impossible? What if you can't imagine ever being the kind of writer you hope to be? How do you practice patience with that?

Easy.

Know that you're wrong.

You're already some kind of writer. You've already experienced times of productivity and joy in your writer's life. You've had moments when you know *it works*. You also know waiting, and you also know disappointment. So you've already experienced the only three states a writer can really experience: triumph, failure, and somewhere in between. It's a fact: Sometimes a writer's life rises—the hope machine pays out—sometimes it falls, and sometimes it just poots along. Whatever state you find it in now, know this for sure: It will change. A writer's life is subject to change.

So at the worst of the worst moments, when writing feels like a hole you can't climb out of, just remember when it wasn't. Reacquaint yourself with a past feeling or experience of triumph, to remind yourself that more such moments lie ahead.

Hope lubricates patience, but hope needs help.

Here's an approach: *Write about your most awesome moment.* Doing this will help by letting you mentally re-enter a time and place where you were on top of the world. Some of that feeling of empowerment is bound to rub off on your here and now.

So what was your most awesome moment? Describe it on paper, to the length of two pages.

In practical terms there are more ordinary moments than awesome moments in a writer's life, so it's good to be in touch with your ordinary moments too. If all goes according to plan, even the ordinary moments will become brighter, more incisive, more completely and consciously realized over time, more successful. Writers get better. Sure they suffer setbacks, but also they grow, as a direct function of the hard work they do. Why? Because for writers, as for characters, the truth is revealed under pressure. Under the pressure of striving toward a better practice of writing, you reveal yourself to yourself as someone working toward that goal. How can you not feel good about that?

We face the same sort of issues over and over again in our writer's lives.

Is this the sort of work I want to be doing?
Will all of this unpaid effort ever pay off?
Am I the only one who feels this way?
Does any of this even matter?

With practice we become better at confronting these issues, just as we become better at typing with practice.

We also get better—*must* get better—at revealing the hidden truths of our own experience. To be a writer, to have an authentic practice of writing, one embarks on a psychological self-study as grueling—and rewarding—as any therapy. Only you don't have to pay $60 an hour for it. All you have to do is tell the truth about you to you.

Simple, huh?

Ha!

There are whole vast sectors of my psyche where I'm simply scared to go. For visualization purposes, I label these sectors "black holes," and imagine that I'm navigating through my mental inner space in some kind of space ship. Conflict-avoider that I am, whenever I encounter these black holes, I'm inclined to navigate around them. However, on some level that makes me angry, because it's my brain—*my turf*—and why should there be places in my own brain where I don't get to go? So I adopt a different strategy. Instead of skirting the black holes, I attack them. It takes a certain suspension of disbelief; I have to pretend that I won't get hurt. But time and again I discover that confronting the black hole doesn't kill me; to the contrary, it kills the black hole, and opens up more of my inner space to me. According to this model, I'm subduing and colonizing my own brain. This makes me feel good, and confident, and it makes me more willing to face the next black hole when I see it.

But I have to face the first one when I see it.

Here's a black hole: I imagine that I'm never going to be a "front of the bookstore" guy. No matter how many books I write, or what kind, I feel that I'll never be the sort of author who's wall-to-walled in massive displays in bookstore windows. I know that this is a negative feeling, and I know that I can either deny it or confront it. If I deny it, it holds hidden power over me. If I confront it, the power is no longer hidden, and then the toxic effect goes away. Okay, maybe I never *will* be a "front of the bookstore" guy. I can still have a practice of writing. I can still be better today than I was yesterday. By confronting my negative feelings, I improve access to my own brain.

Honesty, again, is the baseline requirement. To be the sort of writer you want to be—free in your own head, able to convey real emotion on the page—you must be willing to confront your own black holes honestly and, insofar as possible, fearlessly.

Want to know my black holes? Will you settle for the short list?

> *I should have started writing at an earlier age. I should have finished more of what I started. My peers are more successful than I am. I can't seem to concentrate as well as I'd like to. I wish I'd tried stand-up comedy. I don't work hard enough at selling myself. I don't work hard enough at deepening my philosophy. I just don't work hard enough.*

Oh man, could I go on. But what are your black holes? Don't be afraid to name names.

Truth destroys fear. Hope lubricates patience. So confront fear, have hope and practice patience. Maybe one day the hope machine will pay off big time. Or maybe it never will. Either way, we still get to play, and that, in the end, is really all a writer can ask.

conditionals

If is the liberation word. With *if* you can consider any possibility. With *if*, you can write a *conditional*, a poem of sorts or creative speculation. You can use a conditional to create, link and examine a series of premises or perspectives, with a view toward deeper understanding. Here's a conditional.

> *If you look harder, you see better.*
> *If you see better, you know more.*
> *If you know more, you're smarter.*
> *If you're smarter, you look harder.*
> *If you look harder, you see better.*

If is the liberation word. It allows us to examine any proposition, even perfect sophistry.

> *If the criminals are guilty, they must be prosecuted.*
> *If the criminals are prosecuted, they must be guilty.*

To build a conditional, start with any condition. Let's say it's raining. Next, link the condition to a conclusion.

> *If I go out, I'll get wet.*

Now make that conclusion the subsequent condition.

> *If I get wet . . .*

And draw another conclusion.

> *. . . I'm bumming.*

Keep connecting conditions to conclusions—

> *If I'm bumming, I won't go out.*

—till you find a way to bring it home.

If I don't get out, I won't get wet.

That's a pretty lightweight conditional.

If I go out, I'll get wet.
If I get wet, I'm bumming.
If I'm bumming, I won't go out.
If I don't go out, I won't get wet.

Lightweight conditionals. We warm up on those.

Bask in your cleverness. Once you get past that, you can use conditionals to examine interesting aspects of your writer's life. You'll have a way of holding the glass of your experience up to your own eye. Just remember that the goal is *interesting speculations,* not *valid conclusions.* And the structure above is only a framework. Shape your conditionals according to your own rules. Unlike sonnets, conditionals are . . . highly conditional; you can build them any way you like.

If words have meanings, this sentence makes sense.
If scramble king wang dish, happy flatiron.
If there are rules, then no scramble king wang dish.
If words have no meaning, this sentence makes no sense.

As a writer's tool, conditionals let us think about things we can't think about. They let us confront hidden assumptions and taboos of belief or behavior that hinder the development of our characters, stories, and ideas. If you have a character with a particularly troubling point of view—one you don't validate or agree with in your own life—it can be difficult to write that point of view effectively. Conditionals let you enter and examine that perspective without having to sign on to the truth of it.

Here is the head of a serial killer:

If people annoy or bother me, they must be stupid.
If they're stupid, they deserve to die.
If they deserve to die, then I'm justified in killing them.
If I kill them, they won't annoy or bother me any more.

Now we have a better understanding of the (circular) logic that a serial killer might employ, without ever having to validate the serial killer's approach as right or true in any sense.

Conditionals provide a platform on shaky ground.

Use a conditional to get inside the head of a character you're working with now.

Let's say you have a character whom you're trying to move from denial to acceptance on the theme of *let love in*. You can use conditionals to explore the state of love even if you don't happen to be in it at this time.

If you're afraid of love, you can't open your heart.
If you don't open your heart, you can't let love in.
If you don't let love in, you'll never know if love works.
If love works, you don't have to be afraid.

Or even more simply:

If you're afraid of love, you can't let it work.
If love works, you have nothing to fear.

Is it okay to be afraid of love? A lot of people are. Do you want to be? Most people don't. Since conditionals let you start with something you "know" not to be true, you can explode an assumption and examine the pieces. You *know*, for example, that you're growing older. The absolute fact of this makes it difficult to contemplate *not* growing older.

But it can be done . . . conditionally. I contemplate *not growing older* to make *growing older* easier to contemplate.

If I weren't growing older, I wouldn't fear death.
If I didn't fear death, I'd be free.
If I were free, I'd be eternal.
If I were eternal, I wouldn't grow older.

"If I were free, I'd be eternal." Is this true? Doesn't matter. It's an opinion, a *condition*, which we generate through the application of creativity to structure, and upon which we may now meditate at our leisure.

But sometimes conditionals do speak the truth. They can speak the most direct and meaningful truths about yourself and your writer's life. For me, for instance, I crave approval.

Do you too? *Good for you!*

We can use the conditional structure to examine our relationship with the concept of *approval*.

If I don't have approval, I need it.
If I need approval, I'll go get it.
If I get it, I'll have it.
If I have it, I don't need it.

Does this free us from the need for approval? Of course not. But it gives us better insight into the effect of the need. The following conditional, though, paints a somewhat different picture:

If I have approval, I need more approval.
If I get more, I need more.
If I get more, I need more.
If I get more, I need more . . .

Now we have a one-way conditional, going on and on forever, like π. It ain't ever going to end—not if *have more/need more* is our first condition.

Have more/need more is an addiction condition. How many of those can we name? Substance abuse, sure; bad habits, sure; toxic behaviors. But not all addiction conditions are bad things. We can have a *have more/need more* relationship with achievements, thrills, love, joy, music, movies, books, or even the buzz of pure emotion.

Name the addiction conditions in your life.

Life itself can be viewed as an addiction condition. How stuck are we if we're stuck in this condition?

If I die, it'll be too soon.

But if you can set the condition, you can also change the condition. You can insert any condition you know to be true. You can insert any condition you know to be false.

If I die, it won't be too soon.

This lets you try out new ideas, and gets you unstuck from old ways of thinking. Even if you don't entirely *buy* your new way of thinking, at least it's new, and that's not nothing.

If you write a conditional about yourself, you'll examine your condition.

If you examine your condition, you'll discover something new.

If you discover something new, you'll have faith in your powers of perception.

If you have faith in your powers of perception, your perception improves.

If your perception improves, you examine existing conditions more effectively.

In other words . . .

If you look harder, you see better.

In the practice of writing, that's worth its weight in conditionals.

writing with a partner

Why write with a partner? Here are some pros.

> *More ideas. Externalized motivation.*
> *Mutual support. Higher quality. Greater*
> *output. Division of labor. Complementary*
> *strengths. More professional contacts.*

And here are some more.

And here are some cons.

> *Half the money. Ego risk. Your partner*
> *drives you crazy. Chain is only as strong*
> *as the weakest link. Emotional conflict.*
> *Diversion of time/energy. Possibility of ugly*
> *divorce.*

And, you know, some more.

Did you take the time to list some pros and cons? Look, you only have to play along if you want to, but if you're not prepared to look closely at the relationship between writing partners, you're probably not ready to have one. After all, you wouldn't want a partner like that. You'd want someone alert to the relationship, like you.

Someone who's willing to work hard, not just at writing, but at making the mechanics of a partnership work.

So when you go looking for a partner, go looking for an equal. Someone at your same level of:

- development
- experience
- sensibility
- and work ethic

Find someone who works harder than you do—and find someone who's looking for someone exactly like that. Then you'll have two hustling writers and you can get some real work done. Avoid situations in which one writer hustles while the other one slacks, because the hustling half soon gets resentful and the partnership ends.

Find someone on your wavelength. It's not necessary that you agree on every theme, every plot twist, every character flaw. But when you get down to committing whole hunks of your life to a writing project, you'd better both believe in it deeply, or someone will be frustrated and unhappy before it's done.

Find a partner you like. You're going to be spending a lot of time in a room with this person, so it would be nice if you generally got along and enjoyed each other's company. If yours is an Internet partnership, this is less important, but partners are still part of each other's lives; it's best if partners can also be friends.

Find a partner who takes criticism well; find a partner with self-awareness; find a partner who shares your goals; find a partner with a sense of humor; find a partner who likes to do first drafts; find a partner who shares your tastes; find a partner to learn with; find . . . well, what kind of partner would you like to find?

→

The worst thing about writing with a partner, I think, is this:

You don't get to drive all the time.

Not all the decisions are yours. They can't be. If they are, your partner's not sharing the load. On the other hand, here's this paradox: You like a partner who's strong, because strong equals hard working. But strong also equals stubborn, and when stubborn creativities clash, nobody gets their way completely.

Get used to it. Get used to compromise. Settle on the concept that two writers finding a common vision at a higher level outranks one writer alone in a room doing nothing. Can I sound commie here for a second? *Sacrifice for the common good.* A good partnership pushes itself aggressively through the thicket of compromise toward the common good.

And get used to *no.* Be a partner who can give your partner a good, frank *no*—and take one too. A good, frank *no* can save a tremendous amount of time. Say you pitch your partner an idea for a screenplay based on this vague postulate:

> *What if the constellation Orion's Belt were really a belt, like someone could go around wearing it?*

Your partner gives you this extremely blank look and you realize maybe that's not an idea worth the next six months of your life after all. Isn't that better than wasting the next six months finding out?

Also, a good, frank *no* builds the credibility of *yes*. If two partners have the real experience of saying bluntly to each other, "No, that's not working; no, it's not good enough; no, let's try it again," then when they reach the point where the work *works,* they find that they can trust their judgment.

> *Cripes, we've said no often enough, but*
> *neither of us feels like saying no now.*
> *Guess we've got a real yes here.*
> *Let's move on.*

Obviously this model suggests that both partners are committed to serving the work and not serving their egos. If both writers aren't signed on to serving the work, there's going to be trouble, because the writer in service of the ego has trouble allowing any idea to go forward except his own.

Serve the work or serve the ego; the choice is always yours.

How do you know if your partner is serving the work? Talk about it. Open, honest dialogue *about the writing partnership* is critical to its success. In the middle of mapping out a chase scene, for example, you should be able to step back and say, "You know, we're having good process here because we're building on each other's ideas without having to claim ownership." When your partner gives you another one of those famous blank looks, you can smile inside, knowing that you're tending the team like a garden, like you should.

If you've found someone you think you'd like to be partner with, here's an easy way to take the team out for a test drive. Read each other's work and give each other notes. Make them good, detailed, comprehensive, challenging notes. If your critiques make sense to one another, you'll know you're on the same wavelength. If you can give and receive notes on each other's work without going medieval on each other, there's a shot you can do it on a joint project next.

But don't just jump into this thing. Remember that a writing partner—of necessity—has some access to your inner life. And even if you're ready for that, people around you may feel differently. When time and emotional energy get devoted to a writing partner instead of a spouse, for example, conflict and even jealousy may arise. So take your time, and consult your loved ones, in deciding whether to form a writing partnership. It's not a decision you make in a vacuum.

And take your time discussing the terms of that partnership. Are you together for one project? A series of works? Are you in it for the duration? Will you each continue to work on independent projects, or will you both commit your whole practice of writing to the partnership's goals? And while we're on the subject, what are those goals?

If the partnership bombs, it's not the end of the world. But it can set back a career. Here's an unfairness of Hollywood: If writers have success as a team, and then split up, they both have to start over from scratch. People who read samples of joint work assume that all the good stuff came from the partnership, and not from the writer now sallying forth on her own. Since you can't guarantee that any partnership will hold, you have to be prepared to start over at some point in the future. Again, if you're not prepared to contemplate this possibility, you're not ready for a partnership. But get ready. If you've never done it before, you'll find that the gains of partnership writing outweigh the risks, in experience and learning alone.

The best thing—the very best thing—about writing with a partner is that you have someone to share with. And not just the agony; the ecstasy too. The second best thing about writing with a partner is the powerful externalizing of motivation. Writing to meet a partner's expectations will make you work harder than you might work to meet your own. So give it a shot. You have nothing to lose but your solitude.

writers and editors

"Good, but needs work." That's the only note my first writing teacher ever gave to anyone, and man, it pissed me off. *Wasn't he paying attention?* Then I realized that, for a young writer trying to improve, "Good, but needs work" was pretty much all the edit I needed because my work was always good if it was growing, and it always needed work till it was grown.

Beyond "good, but needs work," though, a writer needs a clear-eyed, forceful, well-informed and articulate editor to help her hone her skills. Of course, needing this thing and wanting this thing are two different things. What we *want* as writers is someone to tell us that every word we've written is brilliant, perfect, pure gold. What we *need* is someone to tell us just the opposite, for the indispensable purpose of closing the gap between the writing we've done and that dim and distant goal of actually having written pure gold.

From working with editors and also working as an editor, I have found that, like a writing partnership, the writer/editor relationship requires honesty, vulnerability, openness and devout service to the work. I believe you can grow by being this kind of writer. I know you could make a living being this kind of editor.

So here's a little writer/editor reference guide, some things to think about as you and your editor get involved. "Good, but needs work" is only the beginning.

THE WRITER/EDITOR RELATIONSHIP
This relationship can trigger approach/avoidance

conflict in both the writer and the editor. The writer wants and needs an editor's input, but fears rejection. The editor wants to help, but dreads being the bearer of bad news.

THE WRITER'S ROLE

Writers do the heavy lifting. They take the material as far as they can on their own, and then turn to an editor for help. The work should be far enough along that the editor can comment meaningfully upon it, but not so far along that everything is set in stone in the writer's mind.

THE EDITOR'S ROLE

Editors find problems. That's their job. Problems in story, characters, jokes, structure, dialogue, thought, intent, clarity, marketability, whatever. Editors tell writers what's working, but mostly they tell them what's not. An editor with nothing but good news is not much use to a writer.

WHEN THE EDITOR IS NOT THE BUYER

When the editor is a writer's (paid or unpaid) advisor, then the writer has the freedom to accept or reject the editor's suggestions. Writers and editors in this relationship should remember that the writer has the final say.

WHEN THE EDITOR IS THE BUYER

When the editor is also the buyer, the situation changes. A writer for hire must be prepared to yield authority with grace. Many writers do not understand this, or resist it for reasons of fear and ego. This can be counter-productive to a writer's career. Not to put too fine a point on it, some of the most valid writing is the signature on the check.

WHAT A WRITER LOOKS FOR IN AN EDITOR

The perfect editor is someone who gives fast, complete, articulate and detailed notes. Writers need editors who can go beyond "I like this" or "that doesn't work" and really get into the specifics of the material. Writers also like editors who can give bad news gently, but this should not be a requisite.

WHAT AN EDITOR LOOKS FOR IN A WRITER

Editors need writers who are flexible, creative, willing to listen, and eager for new ideas. Editors like writers who understand that there's more than one right answer. Above all, editors want writers who serve the work.

GOAL OF THE EDITING PROCESS

At every step, the goal of the editing process should be to improve the material. This is not about judging the work and declaring it good or bad. It's about taking it from where it is to where it potentially can go. Another goal of the process is to *improve the process*, so that the next edit is easier, more informed and more effective than the last.

WHY WRITERS RESIST

Good editors come in with fresh perspectives and give their writers a clear sense of where the material is working and where it's not. Many writers want and need their editor's input, but resist rewriting just the same. Ego is part of it, but a strong desire to *just move on* is probably the controlling emotion. If you're ready to let yourself off the hook before your editor is, *listen to your editor* and stay on the hook a while longer. Your work will be glad you did.

DEALING WITH CRITICISM

Writers taking criticism have a choice of two filters. The "judgement" filter asks, "how does this criticism make me feel?" The "process" filter asks, "how can I use this information to improve what I'm trying to write?" Writers deal effectively with criticism when they absorb information through the process filter, and give the judgement filter the afternoon off.

GIVING NOTES EFFECTIVELY

Editors give effective notes by being detailed, complete and precise, by offering the thoughts behind and the reasons for their opinions. Editors help writers by always making it clear that their mission is simply to help the work reach its best destination.

RECEIVING NOTES PRODUCTIVELY

Writers take notes effectively when they . . . listen. Simply listen. Never argue or explain, just listen. Take the notes on board, and deal with them as a source of information, data and possible solutions to the problems at hand. Never forget that your editor is there to help, not hurt.

SERVING THE WORK VERSUS SERVING THE EGO

For reasons of focus and clarity, it's more productive to serve the work than to defend the ego. Paradoxically, the more a writer serves the work, the better the work becomes. Later, when the work has improved, you feel good. Thus you can actually serve your ego by ignoring it.

THE POINT OF DIMINISHING RETURNS

There comes a point in every project when the time it takes to rework the material is not worth the gains that stand to be achieved. Writers often think this point has arrived before it actually does. Editors are there to see that writers don't quit too soon.

SETTLING FOR 7

Scripts or manuscripts can be evaluated on a scale from 1 to 10, 10 being best. Writers often want to settle for 7, or even delude themselves into thinking that their 7 is really a 10. Great editors, relentless in pursuit of excellence, won't let their writers stop short of authentic 10s . . . or even 11s.

ASKING THE RIGHT KIND OF QUESTIONS

Shrewd editors couch their criticism in questions. For instance, "What emotion are you going for here?" This allows writers to articulate their intention without feeling threatened. Contrast this approach with a statement like, "I don't see any emotion here at all—this is all wrong." That's bound to raise a writer's defenses (and hackles), and from that moment forward progress stops.

BUILDING A FRUITFUL RELATIONSHIP

Writers and editors should take the long view. If all goes well, they'll be working together for years to come, on many different projects. So they should be at least as concerned with having good process (and examining and improving that process) as they are with tackling the task at hand.

WHEN A WRITER GETS TOO CLOSE TO THE WORK

Writers get so close to their work that they can no longer see the problems, or so cozy with their work that they pretend its problems don't exist. A strong editor enforces clarity . . . and reality.

WHEN AN EDITOR OVER-INVESTS IN THE EDIT

Some editors go wrong by becoming more interested in seeing their notes implemented than in seeing the work improve. An editor searching a draft for signs of his own creative input is not serving the writer or the work.

ANGER

Editors frequently have strong emotional reactions to what they read. Often that reaction is anger. Anger at the opportunities the writer has missed, or at a character whose choices or actions leave the editor feeling let down or betrayed. Honest editors don't hide from these feelings, but share them with their writers, because whatever "gut reaction" an editor has, an audience or reader is likely to have as well, and this is the kind of information a writer needs to have.

TYPOS

It's not, strictly speaking, the editor's job to correct typing, spelling and grammatical errors, but it's a nice thing to do. At the same time, writers should be their own copy editors at least.

WHEN WRITERS AND EDITORS FIGHT

Sometimes it gets personal. Writers accuse editors of being stupid or short sighted. Editors accuse writers of being stubborn or lazy or narrow minded. Writers and editors should try to avoid this sort of brawl; the work's tough enough as it is.

ARROGANCE AND INSECURITY

These states of mind haunt many writers, especially ones who haven't dealt with editors much. In service of these emotions, writers will resist editors' suggestions and, in fact, take pains to avoid dealing with editors at all. But writers who say they don't need editors are usually operating from fear and are almost always wrong.

WRITERS AND EDITORS HEAR LINES DIFFERENTLY

Writers "hear" the lines they write in a special way. Characters' voices, even individual words can have nuances known only to the writer. Editors serve writers by not having this special information. They read the work the way a reader will (with virgin eyes) and can evaluate it accordingly.

EDITORS EXTERNALIZE WRITERS' MOTIVATION

A good editor gives a writer a target to shoot for. Writers who cannot motivate themselves often find themselves motivated by their editors' encouragement, insight . . . and deadlines. If you can't drive your own bus, let your editor take the wheel.

EDITORS PROTECT WRITERS

Whatever flaws are present in the work, the writer is much better off if the editor discovers them, as opposed to the potential buyer or publisher or audience or reader. Painful it may be, but *no* from an editor breeds *yes* from the people who count.

HARSH NOTES AND HAPPY ENDINGS

Harsh notes can be hard to take. But at the end of the day, when the material is working and everyone is delirious, the writer has the editor's hard edit to thank. Good is the enemy of the great, and it takes a lot of bad news to make good writing great.

THE GOLDEN RULES OF THE WRITER/EDITOR
RELATIONSHIP
- There's More Than One Right Answer
- There's Always A Better Joke or Line
- Well-Intentioned People Can Disagree
- Don't Make It Personal
- Editors Protect Writers
- Always Make Room For The New Idea
- Avoid Closure As Long As Possible
- Never Give Up!
- Stay Friends
- Save Your Ego For The Awards Ceremony

Can you think of some other useful guidelines for your own writer/editor relationships?

Some writers and editors use abbreviations, acronyms and shorthand expressions to streamline the editing process. This "code" is written on the page of a script or manuscript as a means of transmitting ideas, briefly and effectively, from the editor to the writer. Building a common vocabulary has the benefit of making writers and editors feel like they're allies and not adversaries in the development process. It also makes communication easier, obviously, because the code is commonly understood by both parties. Also, reducing a supposedly negative judgement to an acronym often takes away some of its sting. While it's not the editor's job to make the writer feel safe, it is axiomatic that a confident writer will perform better than one who lives in fear of her own editor's notes. Editors can make their notes less toxic by encoding them in emotionally neutral symbols.

Conscientious writers and editors work together to develop a common vocabulary, and then use that vocabulary to facilitate their work. Over time, you'll develop your own code based on your microculture and shared experience. In the meantime, feel free to use mine. If I were your editor, you could expect to see your script or manuscript annotated with shorthands like these.

- BBB = Blah-Blah-Blah; unnecessary dialogue or unfunny jokes.
- BOD = Bump Or Dump; make more of this moment, or cut it altogether.
- CBB = Could Be Better; a general-purpose challenge to the writer.
- DC = Drinking Coffee; characters are standing around doing nothing. The story is stalled.
- DTD = Done To Death; we've seen this joke or sentiment or setting or plot twist or whatever too many times before.
- IDBT = I Don't Buy This; there's a logic problem here that needs to be addressed.
- LET'S TALK = The problem is too complex for me to address on the page; we need to discuss this point in person.
- MLTP = More Like This, Please; editors use this acronym to point out what they like, and what they'd like to see more of.
- OTN = On The Nose; something's too obvious; bury the intent in the subtext.
- NBB = Need Better Button; find a way to end the scene or sequence more effectively, powerfully or comically.

- NOISE = Material that stalls or clutters a sequence or scene.
- NTBSLT = Not This But Something Like This; you're in the right neighborhood, but this line or joke or thought doesn't quite work.
- RETHINK = Examine this scene or character or moment in light of new information.
- RF = Red Flag; something on the page is so awkward or offensive or illogical or just plain ugly that it stops the reader cold.
- TIGHTEN = Say the same thing more simply and swiftly.
- TDDH = That Dog Don't Hunt; the line or idea or explanation isn't doing what the writer intends it to do.
- YCDB = You Can Do Better; alerts the writer to an instance of weak execution, at the same time reminding her of her personal strengths.

practice practice

When people ask me to consult with them about their writing projects or their careers, the first question I ask is, "Do you have a practice of writing?" I want to know if the writer in question is fiercely and actively engaged in the life-project of mastering this craft. If I hear an answer full of hems and haws, excuses, pre-varications and grand, vague plans for the future, I know that this is not someone with a real writing practice, and I decline to be involved. If I asked you to describe your practice of writing, what sort of answer would you give?

It is so important to have a practice of writing. At the end of the day, nothing else matters. You can be the worst writer in the world, spewing drivel onto the page every day, but if you do it *every day,* eventually it will cease being drivel, or at least evolve into drivel at a higher state. This happens automatically, because if you write, you always improve.

Okay, that might not be true for *every*one. There might be a writer out there somewhere who makes the same mistakes over and over again, spins in the same dervish circles, and never grows as a writer at all. I haven't met that writer yet, but still I'll add this caveat. If you write—and monitor your own process and study your results—you will definitely improve.

Alas, the opposite is also true. If you don't write, you definite won't improve. So that would seem to leave us with a pretty clear choice, wouldn't it? Write, and improve; or don't write, and don't improve. Why is it not that simple? Because the forces of evil are arrayed against the desire to write. Some of these forces are legitimate, and we must honor them. It is a fact, for example, that some writers have jobs, families and other responsibilities that erode their writing time and cut into their active practice. It is a fact that the normal events of a life often intrude; it may be your intention to write today, but if there's a big earthquake in your neighborhood, well, you more or less *have* to deal with that. (And take it from someone who's been through a few, an earthquake can *really* ruin a writer's day.)

You *have* to deal with life; you *want* to deal with writing. To resolve this conflict, make one tiny change. Just make writing something you *have* to deal with too. Commit to the practice of writing. Make it part of your routine, like brushing your teeth. Even if it occupies no more time than brushing your teeth, you'll be moving in the right direction. And soon you'll discover that it occupies a lot more of your time, because writing, like gas, expands to fill the available space. The more hours of writing you put in, the easier and more fulfilling the next hours of writing become. This is axiomatic, and also true.

In the practice of writing, quality is not the major concern. In the practice of writing, the only thing that matters is putting words on the page. In the practice of writing, the only fear is the fear of giving up the practice. In the practice of writing there is joy, because the practice of *the practice* is a goal you can achieve and a triumph you can relish every single day.

So how do you practice *practice*? How can you move yourself by degrees from the kind of writer's life you have to the kind of writer's life you want? Here are my top-ten (okay, eleven) tips.

• PRACTICE PATIENCE. Some days you get a ton done. Some days you don't. You'll tolerate the bad days better if you just *let yourself off the hook*. Stress and pressure are not conducive to good writing practice, so go easy on yourself. Life is long. You do have time.

• PRACTICE IMPATIENCE. If yesterday was a slack day, make damn sure that today isn't. Yes, it's okay to blow off work, but not every day, not if you're serious about your craft. Let yourself off the hook, sure, but put yourself back on too. Demand your own active participation in your active practice of writing.

• SET APPROPRIATE GOALS. Don't imagine that you're going to write a whole novel before breakfast. Do imagine that you're going to do a reasonable amount of work in a reasonable amount of time. Inappropriately large goals kill will and crush productivity. Appropriately small goals, on the other hand, offer the immediate reward of a job, well, done.

• SHOW YOUR WORK. Seize any opportunity to get your words read. Be fearless in this. Recognize that rejection is a natural part of the practice of writing. You don't have to like it, but you do have to accept it. The alternative is a trunk full of stuff that no one sees till you're dead.

• KEEP GIVING THEM YOU UNTIL YOU IS WHAT THEY WANT. The best part of your writing is the part that's unique to you. Your stories. Your style. Your sensibilities. Your ideas. Your way with words. If you compromise your vision, you'll just end up with a compromised vision, which is not only unsatisfying to the writer, but difficult to sell as well. Keep giving them you, even if they keep rejecting you. Eventually—I can't say when and I can't promise soon—your quality will convince them that you is what they want.

• SEIZE YOUR SPACE AND TIME AND TOOLS. It's difficult to have an effective practice of writing in an ineffective space. Do you have a quiet place to work, equipped with a decent computer? If not, make it a priority to acquire these things. Also make your writing *time* a priority. Carve it out of your day, guard it with all due jealousy and don't let anyone—especially you—take it away from you.

• LET YOUR LIFE RISE. The practice of writing is one of deep psychological intrusion. In becoming the writer you wish to be, you naturally undergo major transformations in terms of the person you are. Let these changes take place. As you gather awareness, you improve as a writer; as you improve as a writer, you gather awareness. Let your life rise and your writing will follow.

• USE MAPS. Just as artists use sketches to plan their major works, explore your subject thoroughly before you plunge. Make complete and conscientious outlines of your projects to save yourself the grief of having to abandon mountains of labor when the poor story goes wrong. Maps save time. Is it really so hard to get directions first?

• TEACH. Teach writing. Do it now. The more you teach, the more you learn, because teaching demands clarity, study and investigation of process. And don't imagine that you have nothing to teach; just think about what you already know, and go find someone who doesn't know that but wants to. Then expect to reap the benefits; your own writing will definitely improve. Teach. I swear by this, and always will.

• READ. Read for pleasure or information or inspiration. Read to remind yourself what great writing looks like. Read to assimilate language or style or point of view. Read to steal tricks. In all events, challenge yourself with what you read; if you had never read past *Dick and Jane*, you could never write beyond it either.

• KEEP WRITING. Keep writing, keep writing, keep writing. Even if you hate every word. Even if you burn every page. Eventually you'll stop hating and also stop burning. Quality emerges from quantity. If you just keep writing, you will have an effective and satisfying practice of writing much sooner than you expect.

Writing isn't easy, but it really isn't hard. You put a word on the page, then another and another (and another and another) and soon you have a slew of words on the page. You struggle to encode your thoughts in language, and soon you find that you've encoded effectively; your words are understood. You try to grasp deeper meaning with elegance and power, and by degrees you come to own these things. With time, with patience, with *effort,* the practice of writing emerges from the desire to write. Over time, after much effort, the practice of writing becomes second nature, as much a part of your life as breathing. It's not just a goal you *can* achieve, it's one you certainly *will* achieve if you only keep writing.

writer's block

Writer's block is a *limit*. It limits our productivity, creativity and some other word ending in *-ivity* that I can't call to mind right now. Let's see if we can make this limit limit us less.

Start by studying how you experience writer's block. What are the symptoms of this condition? Mine include:

> *checking my e-mail, staring off into space,*
> *playing computer games, going to matinee*
> *movies, walking the dogs, going for coffee,*
> *doing the laundry, making phone calls*

Yours include:

Now you have a set of behaviors associated with writer's block, activities which fill the time that you'd rather fill writing. What triggers those behaviors? What makes you stop writing and start doing something else instead? Fear. Fear of bad outcomes.

> *If I don't make this page work—this*
> *sonnet, this exercise, this story, this*
> *script—something bad will happen.*

When writer's block is active, we fear bad outcomes. What bad outcomes do you feel will result if you fail to write, or fail to write well?

*People will mock; I'll be wasting my time;
I'll starve and die; my spouse (parent,
sibling, friend, peer) will be disappointed;
I'll have to get a real job; my agent (editor,
reader, audience) will lose respect for me.*

→

Writer's block takes place where fear is present because it's easier to stop writing than to face bad outcomes. To deactivate writer's block, disconnect from bad outcomes. Understand that no matter what happens, today's work cannot have more than one day's impact on your overall state of being.

Writer's block also starts where information ends. When you run out of story or insight or relevant data, when you can't figure out where to go next, writer's block seeps in, bringing frail inertia or deer-in-the-headlights paralysis. It's just flat easier to turn away from a project than to face the task of mining new information.

Consider a project you're currently blocked on. Where do you need more information?

*historical facts, character traits, theme,
detail, world of the story, plot twists,
language*

Writers experience writer's block as a state of *can't create*. Well, if you can't create, investigate. Gather more information. That's something you can always do, and it fights writer's block two ways. It directly adds to what you know about your current writing project. It also makes you feel like you're not just a completely useless waste of space; at least you're doing some research.

Here's a common writer's lament: *I can't figure out where my story goes from here.* And the accompanying feeling is one of despair, what I call SPLS, or Sad Pathetic Loser Syndrome. *I can't figure out this story, so therefore I am a sad pathetic loser.* At this point, you've not only lost the plot, you've also lost confidence. But when you stop writing and start gathering more information, confidence returns. Successful in your quest for new data, you feel productive and proactive. With fresh information and restored confidence, you're ready to resume work.

To defeat writer's block, gather more data.

You can gather data about your story, characters, theme or other subject stuff. You can also gather useful data about how you feel. Study the frame of mind you bring to your work. Do you enter your writing space with authority, or do you tiptoe in? Do you engage the writing process with joy? Where is the focus of your attention?

> *Some days I can concentrate, it seems, for just a minute at a time. Then I'm "out the window," thinking about what my friends are up to, or wondering if the car is due for an oil change soon. Then I cringe at my own indiscipline. Here I am calling myself a writer and I can't even concentrate on the task at hand. Feh!*

It's easy to see which states of mind are helpful to the writing process and which are not. Confidence helps. Doubt doesn't. Precision helps. Vagueness doesn't. Honesty helps. Denial doesn't. You're better off if you can even just say, "Look at this writer's block I'm having now." At least you know what's going on.

What's going on in your mind when writer's block strikes?

Understanding writer's block is a long-term writer's task. But you don't even have to understand it in order to outwit it. All you need are strategies. Here are some I use.

SET DEADLINES. Deadlines beat writer's block like rock beats paper. The strong fear of missing a deadline pushes the weak fear of failure aside. So give yourself deadlines. Fake them, it's okay. A useful fiction is a fiction, but it's useful just the same.

EXTERNALIZE MOTIVATION. If you can't set your own deadlines, get someone to set them for you. Take a class or join a writer's group, or even make a promise of productivity to a spouse or a mentor or friend. Do it for them if you can't do it for you.

PROCRASTINATE LATER. Give the first available moment of your day to writing. The sense of smug self-righteousness you get from *putting writing first* will energize your whole day. Plus, you can't fret all day about not getting around to writing if you got around to it first thing.

SCHEDULE MINI-SESSIONS. Wait to begin writing until just 15 minutes before you absolutely, positively must be somewhere else. Inside this tiny writing window, your expectations are nice and low. Low expectations lull writer's block to sleep. And you'll be surprised by how productive even 15 minutes of real writing can be.

BREAK IT DOWN. Writer's block looms when we see our writing project as a monolithic whole. We cower before its hugeness. Needless to say, it's hard to cower and write at the same time. To make looming things loom less, pick a part, then pick it apart. Keep picking till it gets down to something you can handle.

GENERATE TEXT. Describe in words what you're not able to write right now. In other words, if you can't work on your project, work *around* it. Tell yourself you're not writing, just shopping for detail. But since it *resembles* writing (you are, after all, putting some kind of words on some kind of page), expect to feel better about yourself afterward for merely having engaged in the act.

STEP BACK A STEP. A lot of times what daunts us is the sense of not being ready. Was today the day you planned to go from story to script, yet somehow you find you just can't get started? Then don't start. Spend another day in story. You'll get the benefit of thinking about your story some more, plus you'll maybe get so sick of story that going to script will seem like the lesser of evils tomorrow.

FIDDLE WITH THE FORMAT. Get the busy-work out of the way. For example, I always devote the first day of a script to formatting issues. I set my margins, write macros for the characters' names, fill in the mindless blanks. It feels like writing, but it comes without threat. Before I know it, I've tricked myself right past the block of "script: day one" and into the writing beyond.

WRITE SOMETHING ELSE. If you can't tackle the task at hand, tackle an easier one. Work on a section of your writing project that you understand better and fear less. Look especially for the sections that seem to want to write themselves. What you learn while working on the easy parts will inform your efforts when you go back to the hard parts later.

What strategies do you use to defeat writer's block? What ones *could* you use?

To beat writer's block in the long run, just keep watching yourself work. Be alert to when and how writer's block attacks, and eventually it will stop taking you by surprise. Sheer experience wears away writer's block over time. Maybe you'll never get past it completely, but you'll sure have less of it later on than you did in your rookie years. Just keep writing. Everything follows from that.

q & a

In organizing a writer's life, some questions are bound to arise. Here are a few I've been asked.

WHAT'S THE FIRST RULE OF WRITING?
Write. Now. Write now. Today. Something. Anything. Nothing else matters. Follow this rule and you're a lock to succeed. Write now. That's the first rule. There is no second.

SHOULD I WRITE DOWN MY DREAMS?
Sure. Whether you think your dreams are divine inspiration or the turgid gurglings of your semi-subconscious, it's information either way. My dreams occasionally give me valuable instructions in actual literal words: *"True genius works within form." "You have to control your destiny to fulfill your destiny." "If you have the ability to change your mind, you've already achieved higher consciousness."* I'd have lost this useful guidance if I hadn't written it down. What do your dreams give you?

SHOULD I BE WORKING ON MORE THAN ONE PROJECT AT A TIME?
Yes, for two reasons. First, you maintain momentum. It's easier to keep writing than to start writing, and multiple projects help you never stop writing. Also they help each other out: What you discover in one project may solve a problem you're having in another.

WHY DO I HAVE TO DO REWRITES?
Because that's how the work improves. Because it never starts out as good as it gets. Rewriting is labor at

best, soul killing at worst (because you have to murder favored children.) Throughout the process, there's so much aggravating *waste*. Soldier on . . . the answer is *just 'cause*.

WHAT IF MY READERS AREN'T AS SMART AS ME?

If you're asking should you write down to your audience, I say no. But keep in mind that audiences comprise a bell curve. Some will be too dense to grasp your intent no matter how plain you make it. Others will be too sophisticated for you, no matter how jucily Joycian your prose. I try to write for the big fat middle of the bell curve. Don't write *down to* an audience; do write *for* an audience. But trust your readers; they're generally 10% smarter than you think.

SHOULD I START WITH STORY OR CHARACTER?

Both. Develop your characters to reveal your story and develop your story to reveal your characters. When I'm writing narrative fiction or script, I don't draw much distinction between story and character because I'm going to have to know everything about both before my work can be called complete.

WHAT IS AN APPROPRIATE LEVEL OF DETAIL?

An appropriate level of detail is the amount of information you need *at this stage of development* in order to move productively to the *next stage of development*. As you move through stages, you move naturally from less detail to more detail. The appropriate level of detail is always *more* detail than the last level and *less* detail than the next.

SHOULD I SEND OUT SASEs WITH MY SUBMISSIONS?

Some say yes, but I say no. The stamped, self-addressed

envelope just makes it easier for the buyer to reject what you're selling, and that job's too easy already. Don't send any message to anyone that suggests you have less than absolute faith in your work.

DOES THE FEAR EVER GO AWAY?

Nope. You get better at managing it, tricking it and neutralizing it, but it doesn't vanish or get vanquished. Nor should we expect it to, because we're constantly playing for higher stakes. Whenever we try a new thing, we worry that this will be the time the well runs dry. The good news is that, while fear never goes away, creativity never leaves either.

WHAT'S THE HARDEST PART OF WRITING?

For me, first drafts. Once I'm through the "heavy lifting" of putting a draft on its feet, I feel more secure, cheery and chipper. You may have a different "hardest part," but all of it involves (if you're conscientious) more hours of labor than you'd like it to. The hardest part of writing is writing, and if you're looking for an easy job, this ain't it.

WHY CAN'T I GET TO THE EMOTIONAL CORE OF MY WORK?

A writer fails to attack or penetrate the emotional core of a work for three main reasons: A) the writer has no idea what its emotional core is or B) the writer knows the emotional core but doesn't know how to get there or C) the writer knows the core, knows how to get there, but resists out of laziness or fear. To solve this problem, abandon A, B and C and, alternatively, do D) *write the truth*.

WHAT IS THE BIGGEST PROBLEM FACING YOUNG WRITERS?

Their youth. Young writers think they know everything

and fear they know nothing. This leaves them deeply confused. It's useful to ignore the question of whether you know enough, and simply seek to know more. Youth is a problem we all outgrow.

CAN YOU WRITE A STORY WITH MORE THAN ONE PROTAGONIST?

Sure, but remember that each character is the protagonist of his or her own story, and each story must have its own sound structure and satisfying conclusion. Multiple protagonists can be a large organizational problem, but that's all the problem is: one of organization.

IS IT OKAY NOT TO HAVE FAITH IN AN IDEA?

Sure. And disavowing faith in an idea is a great way of allowing yourself to put it out there for consideration and testing. Try this: Preface an idea you're not sure about with the phrase, "This is just the idea I'm having now." This gives you the emotional distance you need to keep your ego safe while you test drive the idea.

HOW MANY EDITORS DOES A WRITER NEED?

Some people like three: One who loves your work, one who hates it, and one who doesn't know it at all. In practical terms, consider yourself lucky if you can find one talented, inspired and experienced editor to contribute to your work. Think of your editor as a wall you have to climb over to get into the garden beyond.

WHERE DO I FIND SOMEONE TO EDIT MY STUFF?

Look among close cohorts first. Find someone who's invested in your success and will grow a long-term writer/editor relationship with you. Failing that, use other writers as editors, and seek ones who are articulate and detailed in their critiques. Avoid paying for this service if you can.

WHAT'S THE WORST CRITICISM YOU'VE EVER RE-CEIVED?

This came from *Lost Lamb* via e-mail, responding to an invitation to an on-line seminar I was participating in: "Thanks, but no thanks—I really don't see what anyone is going to get out of a session with Mr. Vorhaus. He is a faded has-been who is making a killing circuiting the world telling others how to do what he never did very well in the first place." Hey, if I can take it, you can too.

SHOULD I FOLLOW STRICT ACT STRUCTURE IN MY SCREENPLAY?

Inciting incident . . . midpoint pivot . . . act two break . . . there are a lot of screenplay templates you could follow. Use the ones you find useful, but never forget that a screen story is an organic thing, grown as much as it is built. Let your story determine your structure. If your story is authentically interesting and worthwhile, anchored to a vital and important theme, structure will take care of itself.

WHAT'S THE DIFFERENCE BETWEEN STORY LOGIC AND PLOT LOGIC?

Plot logic is what happens because the writer needs it to happen. Story logic is what the characters do because it makes sense to them to do so. Readers and audiences are most satisfied when the needs of plot logic and story logic are served at the same time.

WHAT DOES IT MEAN TO "SUBTRACT THE WAS?"

The verb "to be" is the simplest, plainest one we have. You can liven up your prose considerably just by subtracting the word "was" wherever it appears, and substituting a more precise or animated verb.

WHY HAVE I NEVER HEARD OF THIS BEFORE?
Because I just made it up, shut up.

HOW HIGH IS SEA LEVEL?
Now you're just being silly.

DOES LIFE INSURANCE WORK?
I'm not listening anymore.

WHAT COLOR IS BLUE?
How did you get my phone number?

DO YOU EVEN KNOW WHAT YOU'RE TALKING ABOUT?
click

CREATIVITY RULES

random access

Here are some strategies for taking yourself by surprise.

Go to a bookshelf or a bookstore. Pull down a book at random. Be coy with yourself and hide your eyes so that you can't see the title. Open it at random and read a sentence at random. Try to guess what kind of book it's from.

Here's a sentence I grabbed at random:

> *Claiming that he had business to take care of in Ohio, Giovanni drove the van to Dayton, where he left Sharon with $80, an old Jeep, and instructions to meet him in Detroit.*

To me that sounds like the novelized version of *Unsolved Mysteries*, or possibly the biography of Sharon Stone. What does it sound like to you? Write down your answer before you read on.

It's actually the description of a marriage scam in *How Con Games Work* by M. Allen Henderson. But it doesn't matter what it *actually* is. The creative challenge here is that of looking at a piece of the puzzle and deciding for yourself what the rest of the puzzle looks like. Try it again with a source of your own.

Now take another book, pick a sentence at random and write it down. Or, here, use one of mine.

> *Stefan took the time to show us how we could help ourselves, giving us exercises to do at home (and gently reminding us to do them when we conveniently forgot).*

Next use your sentence or my sentence as the first sentence of a page of prose or poetry or script.

This tactic has the effect of cheating a familiar tedious question: *Where do I start?* For short stories in particular, it's a useful means of linking creative powers to unexpected springboards.

You can also play random access with random words. First, collect or generate a set of unconnected words and phrases. Here are some I happen to have laying around.

> *sea   shake   bulb   raptor   frost   skinny*

Challenge yourself to use your words or mine in a short piece of prose.

By forcing connections, you move your creativity to previously unexplored places. The story you write using instructions from a car repair manual and the words *ivory, escalation* and *Marymount,* plus the phrases *forest*

for the trees and *chamber of commerce,* could never be derived by any other means. It's a lone address in your vast creativity, and it can only be accessed at random.

What other ways can you think of to randomize your creative process?

Suppose you're a songwriter, but all your songs come out sounding like, "Ain't got no lovin' and I'm feelin' so alone." You're in a rut—a lyric rut. To escape, just build your next lyric from non-rut words. A song containing the words *gnocci, blue Pacific* and *ray gun* will have to go a long way to get to "Ain't got no lovin' and I'm feelin' so alone."

There's a fine line between a groove and a rut. Random access helps keep your ruts groovy.

reconstructive sentencery

We think of sentences like we think of stories—beginning, middle and end. But often they're not that simple.

stunning reversals

Stunning reversals are sentences that mirror themselves, like this one from 18th century philosopher Jo-
seph Jockbert:

> *It is better to debate a question without*
> *settling it than to settle a question without*
> *debating it.*

Or this one from me:

> *You can fight a war without winning it,*
> *but you can't win a war without fighting it.*

Or this one from you:

Stunning reversals offer propositions—not absolutes
. . . food for thought of a certain kind. Maybe you're the
sort of person who believes:

> *Children of abused parents are parents of*
> *abused children.*

Or:

> *It's better to date without marrying than to*
> *marry without dating.*

Stunning reversals give you a chance to examine assertions from at least two different sides. When you decide what you hold true, you discover something about yourself and your values—something you can turn around and use in your work.

Or, alternatively, they can be just fun. This one's for my dog, staring at herself in the mirror:

> *I pause to reflect.*
> *I reflect two paws.*

Create a few stunning reversals.

Inspect your process as you go because . . .

> *The more you know about yourself,*
> *the more self of yours there is to know.*

any questions?

What if you wrote a paragraph of questions? What would that look like? Could you convey meaning in a paragraph like that? What if you tried it now? (What if I gave you *sugar,* as a topic, to help get you started?)

> *Where is the sugar? Why have they put it*
> *away? Don't they know how much I like*
> *sugar? Do they think they can get away*
> *with this? Do they think I'll forget? Do they*
> *think I won't pay them back some day?*
> *Are they having second thoughts now?*
> *Why doesn't that surprise me?*

scanagrams

To make a scanagram, just take any sentence and shuffle the words. The object here is to build a new sentence that makes some kind of sense, altered sense or nonsense. Where do you get your target sentences? Oh, anywhere. You can use quotes: "Mad dogs and Englishmen go out in the noonday sun."

> *The Noonday Sun Dogs, mad Englishmen,*
> *go in and out.*

You can reconfigure conventional wisdom: "People who live in glass houses shouldn't throw stones."

> *People who throw stones shouldn't live in*
> *glass houses.*

→

You can even quote yourself: "This I believe above all other things: A man shall find goodness if goodness he brings."

> *Goodness above! Find a man. If he brings*
> *other things, this goodness shall I believe.*

Or draw from sources of your own.

This game plays in reverse too. Challenge your friends to unscramble your scanagram into known phrases.

Some are easy: "And the zone of immediate unloading is only for loading white passengers."

> *The white zone is for immediate loading*
> *and unloading of passengers only.*

Others are only easy if you know your Eliot: "Shall I wear my bottoms of old? I grow rolled. I grow the old trousers."

> *I grow old, I grow old, I shall wear the*
> *bottoms of my trousers rolled.*

We take so much at face value, which not only restricts our philosophical outlook, but also constricts our creative freedom. Scanagrams have the effect of changing (in a modest way) the sorting system in our brains. By allowing ourselves to re-imagine T.S. Eliot or airport protocol, or even our own prior writings, we open ourselves up to a whole new set of mental experiences. Or, as Waldo Emerson Ralph put it,

> *Little of the hobgoblin is a foolish mind's*
> *consistency.*

no verbs

No verbs. Tough challenge. Awkward style. Like a detective novel . . .

Guy in the dirt. Hand on a gun. All the
way dead. Silence, then sirens, then the
lieutenant. "The departed?"

A cop's nod. "Belly shot, brain shot.
Gangland."

The lieutenant's frown. The brief inspection
and the sad call to the spouse.

Now you.

Take away verbs and you're like a runner wearing
weights. The handicap builds strength. The discoveries
you make in working around self-imposed limits both discipline and expand your creativity. Every time you pose
and solve a difficult problem, you become a better
writer.

Pose and solve a difficult problem.

discovery threshold

Suppose you wrote down only some of the words in
a sentence you conceived. Could someone else make
sense of them? Could it be a code of some kind?

Suppose wrote some words you.
Could make of?
Could be code some?

There's such a thing as a discovery threshold. Give someone enough information and they can solve the puzzle. Don't, and they can't. Consider these randomly subtracted sentences:

> *There's __ thing __ big __ encompasses __*
> *anyone __ ask. __ Useless __ ask, "What*
> *__ question?" __ any __ must __ be __*
> *subset of __ big __ and __ the __ question*
> *__ whole. __ may __ that __ question __ ,*
> *"What __ question?"*

Now unless you're me (which only one of us is) that paragraph doesn't make much (okay, any) sense. But the human brain craves order, and will impose order on chaos, just to make itself feel better about life and everything. If you fill in the blanks in the paragraph, you're bound to come up with something that makes some kind of sense.

Even if it doesn't exactly reflect the original:

> *There's such a thing as the big question,*
> *which encompasses all questions anyone*
> *could ask. It's useless to ask, "What is the*
> *big question?" because any question must*
> *necessarily be a subset of the big question*
> *and not the big question as a whole. It*
> *may be that the big question is, "What is*
> *the big question?"*

To play this game, just take a chunk of text and subtract any parts you wish. Set it aside for a while until you forget what it was originally about. Alternatively, have a friend do the deconstruction, and then you'll *really* have to rebuild from context. You don't have to insert exactly one word in between exactly every two words. Just mold and remold the text, like clay, until it starts to take shape. Let's try it with this news article:

> *To the astronauts' delight, bad weather at NASA's space shuttle landing site in Florida may keep Columbia in orbit an extra day, which would be a record-breaking 17th. "I'm keeping my fingers crossed, my legs crossed, my eyes crossed and everything else I can cross, that that will happen," astronaut Al Sacco said Friday, 14 days into the laboratory research mission. Columbia and its seven astronauts are due to land at Kennedy Space Center on Sunday morning.*

Here's my arbitrary reduction. Feel free to make your own.

> *The delight weather landing Columbia extra 17th. "Fingers, legs, eyes, everything I can happen." Al days laboratory research. Due Kennedy.*

Now let's take this baby out on the test track and see what she can do. You go first.

> *The director expressed her delight as stunt*
> *man-turned-special effects guru Al "Spud"*
> *Webber braved bad weather and pre-dawn*
> *dark to perform his famous "monster*
> *landing" on the set of Columbia's new*
> *movie, STAGE FLIGHT. Webber, who*
> *started as an extra, is in his 17th year as a*
> *stunt man. He says the monster landing is*
> *the riskiest move of all. "I seen guys lose*
> *fingers. I seen guys lose legs. Eyes. Any-*
> *thing can happen." Off the set, Al spends*
> *his days in the "landing laboratory," doing*
> *research. He says that big improvements*
> *on the monster landing are due soon. He*
> *lives in Brentwood with his wife and two*
> *dogs, Canaveral and Kennedy.*

And the reason for this all? Well, it can be fun (I hope you find it fun), but mostly just it takes the brain someplace the brain wouldn't otherwise go. As we've already seen, a certain kind of creativity occurs within constraint. Subtracting and then rebuilding sentences or paragraphs is one sort of constraint.

You could find a religious tract on a bus bench.

> *Then he left them, got back in the boat*
> *and headed for the other side. But the*
> *disciples forgot to pack a lunch. Except for*
> *a single loaf of bread, there wasn't a*
> *crumb in the boat. Jesus warned, "Be very*
> *careful. Keep a sharp eye out for the*
> *contaminating yeast of the Pharisees and*
> *the followers of Herod."*

You could strip it . . .

> *Then he left the boat and headed to lunch, except a single in Jesus warned keep out yeast.*

Then do a rebuild:

> *"Then again," thought Magruder, as he left the boat and headed to lunch, "it's nice to be dating again." Which he hadn't been, except for that exceptionally devout young lady he'd met at a Single-in-Jesus mixer, who warned him to keep out. Same old Magruder: Hope rises faster than yeast.*

Thus does the sublime become ridiculous. The big fear for some creative people is that they'll never come up with *something new* again. Given your willingness to swap sublime for ridiculous, that shouldn't be a problem.

search and destroy

What happens to sentences when we insert words in an arbitrary nonrandom manner? Here I substitute the word *sausage* for the letter *e* in the Lord's Prayer.

> *Now I lay msausage down to slsausagesausagep, I pray thsausage lord my soul to ksausagesausagep. If I should disausage bsausageforsausage I waksausage, I pray the lord my soul to taksausage.*

Substitute for any letter, word or phrase in any block of text. Your word processor's search-and-replace feature makes this exercise a snap.

→

It's a paradox: there's no creativity, yet something is created. And it's so easy. Just plug OPTION A into FRAME B and see what happens. For instance, what if we insert the phrase *Philly cheese steak* after every three letter word in the Gettysburg Address?

> *"Fourscore and Philly cheese steak seven years ago Philly cheese steak, our Philly cheese steak fathers brought forth on this continent a new Philly cheese steak nation, conceived in liberty and Philly cheese steak dedicated to the Philly cheese steak proposition that all Philly cheese steak men Philly cheese steak are Philly cheese steak created equal . . . that we here highly resolve that the Philly cheese steak dead shall not Philly cheese steak have died in vain, that this nation, under God Philly cheese steak, shall have a new Philly cheese steak birth of freedom; and Philly cheese steak that government of the Philly cheese steak people, by the Philly cheese steak people, and Philly cheese steak for Philly cheese steak the Philly cheese steak people shall not Philly cheese steak perish from the Philly cheese steak earth."*

It seems sacrilegious doing horrible things to the Gettysburg Address—like spraying graffiti on the *Mona Lisa*. Of course we wouldn't do that for *real*, but this isn't about what's real. It's about what's created. Give it a whack.

What it boils down to is this: Sentences, like rules, are made to be broken, and the more freedom you grant yourself the more freedom you have.

name that religion

When you grant yourself freedom, you can create anything. Even a religion. And if you think that it's inappropriate to address religion in a book on creative writing, I would just suggest that creative people who can address the tough subjects (like religion, love, fear, sex, death) find the easier subjects, well, easier to address.

So here's a religion that says think for yourself and believe what you believe. It makes no distinction between what you believe and what's true. This religion believes that everything is true. Also the opposite of everything is true. Also it's not. What do you believe?

This religion offers dual citizenship. Even if you practice another religion, you can practice this one too. This religion excludes exclusion. It validates all faiths equally. While it understands that others might disagree, it still breaks out in hives anytime anyone talks about one true path or one true anything. This religion thinks there's more than one true thing. What do you know to be true?

This religion encourages you to make a moral choice. It doesn't care which one. It responsibly assumes that you will assume responsibility. It reckons that you'll do a thing because it's a good idea, not because it's de-manded or commanded. It knows that some people crave imposed standards of behavior, and says, "Fine, impose your own." Think about your standards. Which ones do you impose? Which are imposed upon you?

This religion doesn't use miracles to validate its author-ity. It doesn't much care whether miracles are miracles or just figments of our imagination—they change us either way. This religion is a huge fan of change. It wonders if you've ever experienced a moment of explosive change or even a miracle, and what that was like for you.

This religion has a few commandments.
- Pay attention
- Be generous
- Seek
- Grow

It imagines that you have a few of your own.

This religion has no holy book, but if it did, it sure wouldn't number the chapters. It figures that the sum of all beliefs should read the same in any order. If you wrote a holy book, what would the title be?

This religion doesn't ally itself with imperialist forces, or against them. This religion welcomes converts but doesn't seek them. This religion refuses to announce itself. It doesn't congregate or go door-to-door. It doesn't go armed. It does everything in its power to be without power.

This religion requires no special hats or haircuts or uniforms; it's not that insecure. It doesn't make you sit or stand or kneel, or meditate or sing or even pray. Or even pay. It has no youth outreach program, no colleges, no theme parks. This religion can't package spiritual truth, nor bind it between covers, sell it as a set of audio cassettes, or preach it at revival meetings. It doesn't threaten anyone with hell, but it wonders what hell looks like to you.

And also what you consider sin.

This religion notes with wry amusement that "God" and "I" are the only commonly capitalized English common nouns. It concludes from this that god and i are one.

This religion is for what is appropriate. It thinks we should update our belief systems as often as we update our tools.

What would you call a religion like this? Here are some entries our judges have received so far.

CHURCH OF THE ORTHODOX PARADOX

ABSOLUTE *relativism*

WHOLLY TABERNACLE

sapienism

the church of the evolvi**ng god**

OmniAgnotheism

noncommitarianism

What would you call a religion like this? Send your entries to jv@sprig.com.

SoundOUBTS

A soundOUBT is a code of sorts. You crack it by reading aloud.

> *Ape ledger legions toothy flak otter hew*
> *knighted stakes offer marigold, end toothy*
> *reap up lick fur widget stance, wan asian*
> *on deer gaud width liver cheese end joss*
> *sticks fur owl.*

This is a very hard way to write, but it sure makes
you choose your words carefully. And it make you think
about each and every word you write. Try it and see.
Otherwise put . . .

> *Dish izzy fairy heart weight hew riot,*
> *butted chewer mix hew chew sure worts*
> *scare filly. Ended mix hew tinker bout itch*
> *endeavory wort hew riot. Trite end sea.*

Those so inclined may translate poetry. This . . .

> *Whose woods these are I think I know.*
> *His house is in the village though.*
> *He will not see me stopping here*
> *To watch his woods fill up with snow.*

becomes this . . .

Hews woodsy saw rye thing guy no.
Hiss sausage sin DeVille edge toe.
Iwo naught seemy stan din kir
Due watches worts fillip wits no.

For extra credit, identify the following:

Wad apiece off war kiss ma'am! Hound
opal end raisin! Hound definite end fractal
tea! End farmin' muffin, hound dicks
prescient admiral bull! End ax shun hound
Leika neighin' gel! End apiary hand shun
hound Leika got!

Here are the rules of soundOUBTS.
- Prop heron aim sorrow Kay.
  - *Proper names are okay.*
- Fur in wort sorrow Kay.
  - *Foreign words are okay.*
- Homo nimbs sorrow Kay (ewe sing fore four for, Fourex ample.)
  - *Homonyms are okay (using four for fore, for example.)*
- Nun cents wort Saar *nada* loud ("nimbs," Fourex ample.)
  - *Nonsense words are not allowed ("nimbs," for example.)*
- Clara tea hiss import tent.
  - *Clarity is important*
- Naught reap lacing uh wort hiss trickily fur bitten (leafing "ass hiss" ass hiss, Forex ample.)

- *Not replacing a word is strictly forbidden (leaving "as is" as is, for example.)*
  - Wort sand friezes shoots hound ass mulch Ike duh Eeyore ridge a nail asp pause a boil. Bud . . .
    - *Words and phrases should sound as much like the original as possible, but . . .*
  - Stile Isreali a preachy hated. Triune bialy gaunt.
    - *Style is really appreciated. Try and be elegant.*

Bud white dewy neat drools sin a furs plays? Ant sir: Tomb ache dug aim aura musing. Widowed drools dare hiss con few shun. If pimple canned fig hewer rout duff raze ewer righting, day wound end joy plane. End a few chains drools orbit rarely, pimple becalm forest rated. Bud a few Mecca pizzle at saw ladle jowl engine, pimple my ten joy Solvang hit. Ord hey mite ink ewer wan star craving lunar tick.

> *But why do we need rules in the first place? Answer: To make the game more amusing. Without rules there is confusion. If people can't figure out the phrase you are writing, they won't enjoy playing. And if you change the rules arbitrarily, people become frustrated. But if you make a puzzle that's a little challenging, people might enjoy solving it. Or they might think you were one stark raving lunatic.*

Bud hats purity mulch strew fur inner think hew riot.

> *But that's pretty much true for everything you write.*

End gnaw, Lett's sol Stan Dan sink too gather hour gnash uh null lamp thin:

> Hoe sake hand dew seethe threw dub
> hairy less knight
> ower dub bran parts whee Wadsworth
> SoCal haunt lees dreaming?
> End he raw kits Rhett Clare, dub poms
> purse ding inn heir
> Gay Proust threw duh knight data flak
> wash till their
> José dust hat starts pan gold ban nerdy et
> waif
> ower dull Andover freed Andy hum off
> herb rave?

true fact/bar fact

A big part of the storyteller's job is to create an alternate reality, and then welcome the reader into this world where the "facts" are just constructs of the writer's mind. In this context, lying is an act of creation, and a skill we could stand to get good at. Play true fact/bar fact to bolster your inventiveness.

I have discovered that there are two classes of reality: things that are true and things that sound true in bars late at night. To play this game, you and your companions take turns sharing "facts" you know to be true, or, conversely, true lies.

> In the song "Buffalo Gals Won't You Come
> Out Tonight," the women referred to are
> prostitutes.

Is this a true fact or a bar fact? Within the (typically vague) rules of this game, if you can't decide, you may request more information, which I would be obliged to provide:

> Black cavalrymen in the American west,
> commonly known as "buffalo soldiers,"
> were not allowed to fraternize with white
> prostitutes. So they had their own camp
> followers, and these women became,
> over time, the "buffalo gals" celebrated
> in song.

Players then vote on whether the fact is true. If they guess wrong, you get a point, and if they guess right, they get a point. Points may be redeemed for drinks or for nothing.

This game is a structured excuse to lie. Which of these is true?

> *All mountains higher than 5000 feet contain trace amounts of gold.*

> *A "muddler" is a tiny bat used by bartenders to crush bitters in the bottom of a highball glass when preparing old fashioneds.*

> *The Battle of New Orleans took place three weeks after the treaty concluding the War of 1812 was signed.*

> *Latin ballplayers were not allowed to play in the Negro Leagues.*

> *Cheese doesn't float.*

Which of these is true?

Within the (admittedly vague) rules of the game, anything you've read in a book or a newspaper or magazine, or heard from a reliable or unreliable source is "true," a true fact. (We know that's not true, but let's let it go for now.) Anything you know for sure that you (or someone you know) made up is a bar fact. Here are a few more ground rules to improve the play of the game:

- AVOID "TWEAKING" FACTS

If I said the Battle of New Orleans was fought three weeks after the War of 1812 ended, but it was really only two weeks, I'd be presenting a "tweaked" true fact. Your fact should either be "real," to your knowledge, or completely made up.

- DON'T USE PERSONAL FACTS

If I told you I collected model airplanes in my youth, you'd have no way of guessing whether that's a true fact or not, and what fun would that be?

- DON'T TRY TO SELL AN OBVIOUS LIE

(Even though FDR was never actually elected president.) Remember, a puzzle is only fun if it's challenging to solve.

There's a variation of this game (maybe there is, or maybe I'm just making it up) called Fictionary History, in which you pose a bogus historical event (or cultural phenomenon or anything) and challenge your opponent to explain or describe why it's true. Points are awarded for satisfyingly stylish or clever answers to questions like these:

Which Nordic people explored the Amazon in the 5th century?

How did psychedelic mushrooms contribute to the development of agrarian society?

Who invented "rubbed" scotch, and what is it?

Or these:

Friends say I have no credibility (this is true; you could ask them). They say that I'm so in love with bar facts that I can't be trusted to tell the truth about anything any more. They may be right. But much of the information we're confronted with (and much of the information a writer creates) is not intended to inform, but rather to convince or manipulate. True fact/bar fact reminds us that reality is subjective: What you see depends on where you stand.

creativity *rules!*

Even when you're not writing, you're writing. Your life is an act of creation when creativity rules.

found art

I had a writing instructor with a notebook fetish. "Carry it with you everywhere!" she counseled. "Write everything down!" In doing so, I found that the world around me generated much useful day-to-day *inventiveness*. And so, rather than tax my imagination, I have become accustomed to borrowing from what's real, collecting and storing the casual creative gifts of everyday life.

For instance, I collect spelling miscues. Here are two from shops in my neighborhood:

FREE FAMILY PLANING

And . . .

REBUILT CATALYTIC COVERTERS

This relic comes to us by way of Amsterdam.

MARIHUANA Our Chocolate Milk contains 0.5 gram Biological Marihuana. We recommended for the best result, the next way of working: Take a Cup or basin, put the contents of the bag in it, and add water or milk to it, after +/- 30 min. you begin to feel the effect. Enjoy the enjoyable light "high", not as uncontrollable as by smoking or eating a space cake. Much pleasure.

Warning: Contains no TAR and NICOTINE

And this . . . I don't even know where this came from. It's just a list of words and phrases—but what an unexpected list. I doubt I could generate such a collection by design.

ACEPHALOUS WITHOUT A RULER FORMLESS
BITTER STERILIZED ADVENTITIOUS ACCIDENTAL EXCITING
DEEPLY RELIGIOUS OPPORTUNE AFFERENT
LEADING TO A CENTER TIMID REMOVING UNAFFECTED
AFFLATUS INSPIRATION EGOISM NOTORIETY GASTRIC AILMENT
AMPERSAND THE SYMBOL & ELECTRICAL MATERIAL
GLASS-GRINDING TOOL FIGURE OF SPEECH ANALEPTIC
RESTORATIVE INSECT GROUP FOOLISH ACTION
MILITARY EXPEDITION ANODYNE SOOTHING MEDICINE
TERMINAL OF BATTERY BOOK OF NOTES KNOTTED ROPE
APPETENCY CRAVING CAPABILITY RIVALRY GLAMOUR ATRABILIOUS
MELANCHOLY HEINOUS RESENTFUL UNGRATEFUL AUSCULTATION
ACT OF LISTENING ACT OF VIBRATING ACT OF KISSING
ACT OF HIDING AUTOCHTHONOUS NATIVE

It's in the nature of found art to be *found*. What have you found just lying around?

800 roulette

Did you know that you can play 800 roulette? Just dial 1-800 numbers at random. It's fascinating what you can find out about American enterprise, plus it's free. And why bother? Just for the sake of gathering information you couldn't gather any other way. I now know, for example, that the Balloon Cocoon ships wholesale balloons out of Dayton, Ohio, but won't ship out of state. Something about distributorship turf, I gather.

The most astounding knowledge is only a phone call away.

➜

The willingness to play this sort of game makes you a friskier person, and a friskier person is a friskier writer in turn. Plus, your writing is unique as a function of the special information you possess which no other writer has. Can you honestly say you have all the information you need? So what are you waiting for? Pick up the phone and dial today!

what beats what?

You've played, I'm sure, the game of rock-paper-scissors, where rock beats scissors, scissors beats paper, and paper beats rock. I confess I've never quite understood the logic of that; from where I sit, rock beats everything. But such is the nature of consensus reality. People think that wrapping paper around a rock defeats it somehow, and so that's how the game is played.

But I know one group whose microculture includes a variation of this game called bear-ninja-cowboy, where bear beats ninja, ninja beats cowboy, and cowboy beats bear. It's a whole-body sport almost, attended by elaborate karate kicks, imaginary gunplay and great gaping growls. In their consensus reality, acting out the roles is half the fun of the game.

I've also heard of cat-tinfoil-microwave, where cat beats tinfoil, tinfoil beats microwave, and microwave most definitely beats cat. You can play this one over the phone because it's all sounds—meow, crackle and hum—and no physical gestures at all.

Everything stands in relation to something, so challenge your inventiveness and create a new version of rock-paper-scissors with its own action-icons and under-lying logic. I give you fire-sponge-water, where fire beats sponge, sponge beats water, and water beats fire. What beats what in your world?

playing "dead"

This one's good for mental dexterity in a car or any place where more than one person is killing time. Playing in turn, try to be the last one using a common phrase containing a certain key word. For instance, if you're playing "dead," then you'd use such phrases as *dead certain, dead calm, drop dead, better dead than red,* etc., until only one person can continue. Then switch to "art" or "jack" or "time" or

Okay, let's play "life." I'll go first.

> *life insurance, life as we know it, life is for the living, lifeline, matter of life and death, secret life of plants, opportunity of a lifetime, life and limb, life science, life cycle, art imitates life, life of Riley, life with father, one life to live, jaws of life, life and times, Life Magazine, Lifestyles of the Rich and Famous...*

It's going to be a long car ride, I can tell.

partnerary litership

What if every famous writer had a famous writer for a partner? What would those collaborations look like? Would Kurt Vonnegut, Jr., and J.D. Salinger write *Slaughterhouse Rye*? Would Anne Frank and Oscar Wilde write *Diary of Dorian Gray?* What title would William Burroughs together with Edgar Rice Burroughs produce? Or Lewis Carroll and Jack Kerouac? Or . . .

As a bizarro party game, propose a partnership of literary titans and challenge your opponents to conceive that partnership's output. As usual in these games, style counts for everything, scoring is nonexistent, and most fun wins. Sure it's a game for lit wonks. Nevertheless, it's a challenge to the wit; plus you can play in reverse.

> *Who wrote* The Scarlet Pooh*? Who wrote*
> The Call of the Wasteland*? Who wrote* A
> Tale of Two Cities and the Sea*?*

When your wit fails you, add a *third* literary luminary, and make it a toss-up question. For instance, if you find no joy in James Joyce plus J.R.R. Tolkein, add Herman Melville and throw it to the crowd. See who can get to a (fun, funny or thought-provoking) solution first.

> *Lord of the Dubliner's Dick?*

trivia for idiots

In these politically correct times, no one wants to feel disenabled about anything. Thus we have trivia for idiots, the trivia game that everyone can play and no one can possibly lose. Scoring is easy: The more you get right, the better you do.

- CINEMA
  In the movie Strangers on a Train, what was the prior existing relationship of the protagonists, and where did the meet?

- GEOGRAPHY
  Bordeaux wines come from what grape-growing region of France?

- MUSIC
  Which ex-Beatle recorded the self-titled solo album McCartney?

- HISTORY
  In his famous, "I shall return," speech in the Philippines, what did General Douglas MacArthur promise to do?

- TELEVISION
  How much money did the Six Million Dollar Man cost?

- SCIENCE
  What are you unlikely to find above the tree line?

The object of this game is not to come up with the answers but rather the questions (and send them to me, for I collect them). There's something so satisfying about crafting a question so craftily self-evident. It's not as easy as it looks.

→

- FINAL SUPER BONUS QUESTION
  *For what class of mentally challenged
  people is trivia for idiots intended?*

once and future

Here's a short list of things that didn't exist 40 years
ago. Not only didn't they exist, they were beyond the
imagining of most people.

> *microwave ovens, voice mail, e-mail,
> cordless screwdrivers, videotape recorders,
> personal computers, compact disc players,
> touch-tone telephones*

Lengthen that list.

→

Now (and here's the hard part) write a list of things
that you think will be commonplace in 40 years. Try to
think of things you can't even think of.

> *Brain augmentation surgery, suborbital
> transport, organ farms, virtual venues,
> subcutaneous computers, something that
> makes my CDs (and what follows them,
> and what follows them) obsolete*

→

This is an exercise in conceiving the inconceivable, something writers do every day.

photo op

To have a brand new creative experience, just follow these simple steps.

1. Get a camera,
2. load it with film,
3. take it out somewhere,
4. shoot the whole roll,
5. have the pictures developed,
6. then sit down and write about them.

You don't have to be a photographer to take photographs.

You don't have to be a writer to write.

employment history

List some (most? all?) of the jobs you've held. I'll go first.

> *mime; Santa on stilts; copywriter; television scriptwriter; temp typist; shoe salesman; flogger of stereos; vendor of records; scooper of ice cream; anagram seller; writer of questions for "Jeopardy" on-line; face painter; poker room management consult-ant; singer/songwriter; ventriloquist; maker of t-shirts and bumper stickers; university lecturer; writer of comic columns for the* L.A. Times; *jingle writer; camp counselor; script consultant; writer of intros to bad movies on video; stand-up comedy writer for a 12-year-old girl; ad manager for a car dealership; babysitter; public speaker.*

You learn something about your history from a list like this. I learn that I've never made money with my muscles. I've never worked long hours outdoors. I've never manipulated money for a living. Except for six months scooping ice cream, I've never served food. I haven't worked in sales since college. Teaching, writing and performing dominate my résumé. What dominates yours? What does your work history tell you about you?

What does your history tell you about your future?

When we're free to choose our profession, we choose something we enjoy, but also something we feel gives us a competitive advantage, to make earning a living somewhat easier. I gave up being a folk singer because I couldn't sing and play guitar all that well. But I could write all right, so I took that up instead.

Doing what you love is the biggest competitive advantage of all, because it keeps you on the course until you win. If you don't love writing—the sheer act of putting words on the page—you're probably not where you belong.

I've often been not where I belong. In high school I worked at the Record King, and man, I didn't belong there. Part of my job included writing prices on little orange stickers and sticking them on the LPs. Every once in a while, instead of $5.99 or $6.99, I'd write **FREE**! on the little orange sticker.

These were not dogs, either. These were popular sides. I'd get people flipping through the bins and then just flipping out. **FREE**? "How come this record is **FREE**?" They'd walk 'em up to the counter and ask me, "Is this right? Is this record really **FREE**?"

"Yep," I'd say, "**FREE**! Enjoy!"

Of course I got caught; and of course I got fired. I supposed I used adolescent anarchy as my excuse at the time, or maybe I thought I was upending conventional reality. Really I was just trying to get fired, at a time when I was brave enough to make mischief, but not brave enough to quit.

What job did you get fired from and why?

True or false: Wasn't it the best thing that could have happened to you after all? Now describe your dream job.

That gives you something to shoot for.

whole-life résumé

Your résumé lists the jobs you've held; your whole-life résumé archives the experiences you've had: the choice, cherished, peak experiences that have made your life rise or, at minimum, defined you to you. Here's a partial listing from my whole-life résumé.

> *went skydiving; won a gold medal at the World Ultimate Frisbee Championships; published some books; recruited and trained New Zealand's first generation of situation-comedy writers; won a poker tournament; got married*

But I'm a whole lot less interested in my whole-life résumé than I am in yours. What will you look back on when your life is done and say, *"That. That made the whole thing worthwhile"*?

Just like your employment history shows you how you've spent your working hours, your whole-life résumé reveals how you've spent your heart. It's an area worthy of examination. Your peak experiences are often your own best springboard to story.

backword

Well, that was a long book. The longest I've ever written, though not, if all goes according to scheme, the longest I'll ever write. The next one will be bigger and, one hopes, better than this. Then again, comparisons are odious, so I'll try to be still in my mind and accept the premise that this book is *exactly as good as it is,* and that the next one will be exactly the same. That seems like a good, safe strategy. It should, at least, protect me from the slings and arrows of negative reviews or (heaven forfend) flat sales.

Do you know that my spellchecker does not recognize "forfend" as a word? So certain was it in its squiggly-red-linedness that I had to open a (book style) dictionary to make sure that I was right about the spelling and meaning of forfend, and, in fact, about its very existence. Well, in one of those tiny blessed moments that gets scattered through a life, I opened the dictionary to the *exact page* on which the word "forfend" appears (and I was right, it is a word, and it means what I think it means.) Has that ever happened to you? Where you open the dictionary or almanac or telephone book to the exact page you want? Okay, it's not a big deal. But it's not nothing either.

We get lucky all the time. We find pennies lying on the ground. We turn back to our television program at the exact instant that the commercial ends. Movies we expected to hate turn out to be small gems. Our favorite products go on sale. People give us love. Some people call this stuff good fortune or coincidence. I just think it's the stuff that's scattered through life, and the more you notice it and see it and cherish it, the more of it that gets scattered toward you.

The same is true for what we write. Despite bleak moments when we're certain that it *all sucks,* it doesn't all suck, and sometimes the stuff that sucks the least is the unexpected gift of creation that comes from . . . I don't know . . . Creative Gift Land. I'm not sure that we can attract more of these creative freebies any more than we can control the actual number of pennies on the ground. But we can (in the case of pennies) open our eyes, and we can (in the case of writing) open our hearts. A creative soul that's prepared to accept creative gifts is much more likely to receive them.

And how do you prepare for gifts? By training hard. By practicing your craft. By improving your perception, so that you'll recognize the gifts as gifts when you see them. Most of all, just by writing, by staying actively involved in the time and the place and the circumstance where such gifts are likely to be found. Write. Just write. Everything follows from that, including the gifts.

So write. Just write. Write what your heart commands or write what the market demands. Write fiction or philosophy or snappy one-liners. Write for the next ten minutes or write for the next ten years. Write for your peers or your children or people you don't even know. Write because you must. Write because you can. And when you're done writing, *share* what you write. Don't hide it away, in a file or a foot locker just because you're afraid somebody won't like it. Trust me on this one, somebody *won't* like it. But someone else will; more to the point, they will be moved or touched or entertained or informed by what you've written, and in that moment the transaction between writer and reader is complete.

Just like this one is now.

Write. Turn your creativity into words like alchemists turn lead into gold. Because creativity rules, and when you use yours, then you rule too.

three parts fluff (an appendix)

1. simile fever spreads like wildfire

It was a small cafe, old as the hills but neat as a pin, clean as a whistle and comfortable as an old shoe. I studied the menu with eyes as big as saucers, for the expression "hungry as a horse" fit me like a glove.

Then, sudden as a summer rain, she walked in, cool as a cucumber and fresh as a daisy. My hunger fled like a bat out of hell. She was pretty as a picture and cute as a button, with skin as smooth as a baby's behind and lips as red as a red, red rose. I knew as sure as I'm standing here that she was innocent as a lamb, chaste as a nun, pure as the driven snow. In an instant, my destiny was clear as a bell, my fate plain as day. We couldn't be just like two ships passing in the night. We had to be thick as thieves.

Quick as a wink, or even greased lightning, I crossed to where she stood. My mouth was dry as a bone. I shook like a leaf and sweated like a pig. You'd have to be blind as a bat not to see that I was drunk as a lord with love. "I may not be smart as a whip or wise as an owl," I said, feeling nervous as a bridegroom and naked as a jaybird, "or sharp as a tack with a mind like a steel trap. I may not be fit as a fiddle or sober as a judge, but my heart is as big as all outdoors. I'd be pleased as punch if only you'd be mine." Loose as a goose, I rambled on. "Marry me," I said. "I'll make you as happy as a hot dog at a vegetarian barbecue."

Her face lit up like a Christmas tree. She said it would be easy as pie to love me if only she were free as a bird, but she had a boyfriend big as a house and mean as a junkyard dog. Then she cried, and her tears fell like rain. Well, I couldn't just sit there like a bump on a log. I stood up straight as an arrow and stiff as a board.

"Bring him on," I said. "I'll make him hurt like the dickens!" Suddenly, like a bolt from the blue, I heard a voice as cold as ice and black as midnight threatening to beat me like a drum. Slow as molasses, I turned around. My heart sank like a stone. He was tall as a tree, crooked as a snake, dumb as a post, ugly as sin and built like a brick . . . well, built like something commonly built out of bricks.

I should have been scared, but instead I felt light as a feather, high as a kite, giddy as a school boy. "Look," I told him, "we're different as night and day. You're strong as an ox and I'm weak as a kitten. Beating me up would be like taking candy from a baby. But I'm stubborn as a mule. Though you may pound me flat as a pancake, I'll still be right as rain because my love is solid as a rock and as deep as the deep blue sea."

Well, that made him mad as a wet hen, or a hornet, a hatter, or even a March hare. He came at me like a house afire, but I was slippery as an eel, slick as a whistle. He found out that catching me was like shoveling smoke or nailing jelly to the wall. Oh he landed a few punches, but they were like water off a duck's back. Soon it became plain as the nose on his face that his great romance was dead as a doornail. That made him hot as hell, but he had to face the fact: sure as taxes, I had won.

Ever since that night, my darling and I have been like two peas in a pod, happy as a lark, or even a clam, with a love as good as gold and a future as bright as the sun.

I'm as proud as a peacock to call her my own. It hasn't always been easy, not like falling off a log. For one thing, we're poor as church mice and sometimes that makes us fight like cats and dogs. So I keep myself busy as a beaver working like a dog to make us rich as Croesus, and when I come home every day, regular as clockwork, she makes me feel as snug as a bug in a rug. Friends call us crazy, and maybe they're right.

Crazy like a fox I'd say.

2. writing in the passive voice should not be done by you

When I was in ninth grade, I loved my English teacher. I had a crush so hard I threatened to implode every time I walked into her classroom. She was Miss White then, but later became Mrs. Mulberry and broke my heart. Miss White taught me two crucial things that year. One, obviously, was don't fall in love with older women who will thoughtlessly get married, change their names and break your heart. The other lesson was this: Don't write in the passive voice.

Passive voice writing is writing that should never be done by you. In active writing, people or things do things to other things or people. In passive writing, things are done to by people or things. Get it? Me neither. But yesterday I was cleaning out the garage and I came across an essay I wrote in ninth grade. A twisted love-tome in the passive voice.

> *The room was walked into by me. Presence in the room was had by Miss White. Greetings were exchanged. Homework*

assignments were handed over by me to
her. A moment of silence took place.
Accusatory eye contact was made. Turning
was done by Miss White, and a reddening
of the face. The blackboard was written
upon by her, the words, "The following
assignment is had by the class . . ."
Awkwardness and hot embarrassment
were felt by me.

"News has been heard by me," was
said by me, "that leaving soon will be
done by you."

"Truth is had by you," was said by her.
"Marrying soon will be done by me."

"Is he loved by you?"

"He is loved by me."

"Congratulations then are offered from
me to you," was said by me, as my cheek
was stained by hot tears from which my
eyes were falling . . .

I stopped reading. "From which my eyes were falling?" How can eyes fall from tears? I shrugged and
skipped down to the end. Apparently, a reversal of fortune had been engineered by me.

The desired effect was had by the caress of
my hand upon the skin of Miss White. A
slumping of her shoulders was done. The
falling of tears of her own took place. A
hugging happened.

"A terrible mistake has been made by
me," was said by she. "Loving of you is
done by me, not him."

"Wait," was said by me, "is it meant by you that loving of him is not done by you, or is it meant that loving of me is not done by him? Understanding is eluded by me."

"Loving of him is not done by me, damn it!" was cried by she. "This life belonging to me has been ruined by me!"

"Hope is still had!" was protested by me. "Running away together can be done by us!"

"Is truth being said by you?" was asked by her through the sniffling of tears. "Will having of me be done by you despite betrayal of you having been done by me?"

A nod was nodded by me. "Let coming with me be done by you," was said by me. "Waiting for us outside is being done by the bike of mine. Riding on the back can be done by you."

Upon the face of her was seen great joy. Leaving took place. And living happily ever after was done by us.

You know, in a perfect world, I'd never have to stand in my garage reading the haunted ravings of a hormonally enraged adolescent. I'd have had the good sense to throw them away long ago. Then again, in a perfect world Miss White would have fallen in love with me and we could have been together. But this is not a perfect world, so all I have are the memories. And a hope. A hope that regret is felt by her.

It is certainly felt by me.

3. not just another pretty phrase

My grandfather grew up in one of those quaint European countries that don't exactly exist any more, and while he never quite mastered the English language, he was always an ardent fan. Or, as he once put it, an eager beagle.

In my grandfather's world, if you got in trouble, you were up a creek without a puddle. If you admired someone, you'd want to follow suit in their footsteps. If you were odd, you stuck out like a green thumb. When he wanted to examine something closely he'd go over it with a fine toothbrush. If you were a good person, he'd call you a diamond in the rut. An achievement was a feather in your nest.

Of all his grandchildren, I think I was his favorite. He used to call me a chip off the old shoulder. We were close, he'd say, like two peas in a pot, through fast and famine, come hell or hot water. Still, he was always warning me not to get too big for my bridges. Which bridges I'd no doubt burn when I came to them.

He greatly admired JFK, whom he described as head and shoulders above water, and not just a flash in the can. He was proud to say that he supported the man long before everyone else jumped on the bandstand. He liked movies that kept him on the edge of his teeth, but hated ones that fell apart at the scenes. And when he loved a song, he loved it all: hook, line and singer.

He had a knack, that man. He could kill two birds with one bush, make a mountain out of a manhole, vanish into thin ice, whip up a tempest in a teaspoon, and pull the wood over people's eyes. He's the only man I know who could have his cake and take it too. He kept his ear to the grindstone and his nose on the ball. A hard-working man, he never rode the gravy boat. Nor would he cut off his nose to split his face.

He was proud to say he pulled his own leg in this world. Beggars, he noted, can't be cheaters. They shouldn't act so high and dry. Just the same, he was always ready to roll out the magic carpet for company. Even his no-good brother, who could eat him out of house and garden, and of whom he often said, "A fool and his money are soon partners."

When he met his wife ("the ol' ball 'n' socket"), it was love at first base. They were poor but happy, living from hand to hand. Later, though, she became a milestone around his neck. He said she left a lot to be despised. Apparently they were like oil and vinegar together.

As he grew older he was fond of saying that he was no springing chicken and, furthermore, not longing for this world. He wasn't trying to make a slick purse out of a sow's ear or glide the lily; he could just read the writing on the wallpaper, that's all.

And now he's passed on. Having kissed the bucket and bidden the dust, he's pulling up daisies, out of his miniseries at last. Things are quiet now that he's gone, so quiet you can hear a pin cushion. And when I find myself missing him most, I remind myself that there's no use crying over malted milk, or, for that matter, beating a deaf horse. It's just the dark before the storm. Rome wasn't burnt in a day. I tell myself these things and I start to feel better.

Guess I'm just a chip off the old shoulder after all.